Detachment and the Writing of History:

Essays and Letters of Carl L. Becker

Detachment and the Writing of History:
Essays and Letters of Carl L. Becker

Edited by PHIL L. SNYDER

GREENWOOD PRESS, PUBLISHERS
WESTPORT, CONNECTICUT

The Library of Congress has catalogued this publication as follows:

Library of Congress Cataloging in Publication Data

Becker, Carl Lotus, 1873-1945.
    Detachment and the writing of history.

    1. Historiography--Addresses, essays, lectures.
I. Title.
[D13.B38 1972]   907'.2   70-152590
ISBN 0-8371-6023-5

Contents

Prefatory Note

OF the essays and letters brought together in this volume only one has appeared in a book before, and several have never been published in any form. The exception, "The Dilemma of Liberals in Our Time," as originally printed omitted the historical outline and its sharp analysis of historical forces leading toward conformity and anti-intellectualism in the masses, themes much stressed in recent sociological studies. This essay in its longer version gains added interest as a document of the year 1932.

The essays on history included here supplement particularly those in *Everyman His Own Historian* and also Becker's book *The Heavenly City of the Eighteenth-Century Philosophers*. It would, of course, be misleading to select any one of the historical essays as summing up Becker's relativism; all of Becker's writing would have to be considered in this connection. "Detachment and the Writing of History," for example, is Becker's earliest substantial statement on historical relativism. The mature Becker would doubtless have revised it, but not, I think,

in any fundamental respect.[1] "Detachment" outlined
views on the nature of historical truth which were a part
of Becker's mature position on history and its relationship
to life and thought. The essay "What Are Historical
Facts?" was designed to provoke discussion at the 1926
meeting of the American Historical Association, and
Becker declared in 1940 that it did not accurately repre-
sent his considered views on history.[2] Nevertheless, the
essay is valuable in itself as well as important in the history of Becker's thought. Those interested in Becker's
views on education should not miss his essay "The Cornell
Tradition: Freedom and Responsibility," in *Cornell University: Founders and the Founding* (Ithaca, N.Y.: Cornell University Press, 1943).

For a treatment of Becker's ideas on history, with some
biographical emphasis, the reader should consult Char-
lotte Watkins Smith's *Carl Becker: On History and the
Climate of Opinion* (Ithaca, N.Y.: Cornell University
Press, 1956). Also of importance is David F. Hawke's
"Carl L. Becker" (unpublished Master's thesis, University
of Wisconsin, 1950). Hawke's study includes an almost
complete bibliography of Becker's writings. The influence
of World War I on Becker's thought is assessed in the
writer's "Carl L. Becker and the Great War: A Crisis for
a Humane Intelligence," *Western Political Quarterly,* IX

---

[1] On the reverse side of the last page of the manuscript of his
comparative review of Benedetto Croce's *History: Its Theory and
Practice* and James Harvey Robinson's *The Mind in the Making,*
Becker has what was probably a tentative list of essays for inclusion
in *Everyman His Own Historian.* "Detachment" is included in the
list but with the notation "Revised."

[2] Becker to Carl Horwich, May 8, 1940.

(March 1956), 1–10. Other studies of Becker are under way.

Becker almost never saved copies of his own letters. Those that are printed in this book have been collected from the persons to whom they were written. It is hoped that Becker's other correspondents will add to the Becker papers by contributing their letters to the Collection of Regional History and University Archives, Cornell University.

I wish to acknowledge the suggestion by Harry Elmer Barnes which was the genesis of this book.

PHIL L. SNYDER

Fullerton, California
April 1958

Introduction

CARL LOTUS BECKER was born in Blackhawk County, Iowa, September 7, 1873. He was graduated in 1896 from the University of Wisconsin and continued there his study of American history under the direction of Frederick Jackson Turner. His doctorate was conferred in 1907. He became an instructor in history at Pennsylvania State College in 1899 and at Dartmouth in 1901. In 1902 he went to the University of Kansas, where he remained until 1916, and after a year as professor of history at the University of Minnesota he became professor of modern European history at Cornell University. He held the latter position until his retirement in 1941. In addition he held lectureships at several other universities: the Storrs Lectureship at Yale, which occasioned his most widely known book, *The Heavenly City of the Eighteenth-Century Philosophers,* at Stanford University, at the University of Virginia, and, after his retirement, at Cornell and at the University of Michigan. He was connected during several years with the editorial board of the *Yale Review,* for which he wrote a number of essays. These, along with his lectures, were collected or

were revised and expanded in the volumes published in his later years. He died in Ithaca on April 10, 1945.

The abiding interest in Becker's historical writing grows from three of its characteristics. First, far more than most academic historians, Becker was a literary artist, and all his published work has the charm conveyed by a fine prose style. Second, and again far more than most writers of history, he had and continually tried to clarify and express a rational conception or philosophy of historical writing—the purposes which should guide it and which might set the standard of its excellence. Third, Becker's personality included and his writing exemplified a broad and keen intellectual curiosity, enlightened by wit and irony and united with a deep moral conviction of the seriousness of the historian's calling and of the significance of history for a truly civilized society.

Becker's concern for the literary artistry of his work is well exemplified in the lecture "The Art of Writing" included in this collection. As he here explains, the mastery of this art was a boyhood ambition and a guiding purpose of his college course. It was thus a purpose long prior in time to his interest in history, and all his life the latter remained in some degree a medium for accomplishing that purpose. Again and again throughout his life he returned to the question of what constitutes good writing, and in the lecture he states what remained his mature judgment on the matter. Good writing is a perfect union of form and content in which language becomes a transparent medium for conveying the writer's thought, emotion, or purpose. Bad writing, on the contrary, consists in an awkward, ambiguous, or imperfect expression of meaning, or equally in permitting the mode of expression

to become a mere adornment or a distraction from the meaning.

The good style is the style that is suited for expressing whatever it is—matter of fact, idea, emotion—that in the particular instance needs to be expressed: "proper words in proper places." [1]

A study of the repeated revisions and amendments to which Becker submitted his own manuscript proves that this was indeed the ideal which he sought. The grace and felicity of the finished product—enlightened to be sure by his inimitable wit—depends in no small degree on his attainment of the ideal.

In the second place, however, this idea of good literary style was in no sense extraneous to Becker's idea of his work as a historian. For good history as he understood it includes both mastery of fact and imaginative interpretation; it is both a science and an art. This conception of history, stated and developed in many earlier essays, notably in his Presidential Address to the American Historical Association, "Everyman His Own Historian," is exemplified in the essay entitled "What Is Historiography?"

His [the historian's] object would be to reconstruct, and by imaginative insight and aesthetic understanding make live again, that pattern of events occurring in distant places and times past which, in successive periods, men have been able to form a picture of when contemplating themselves and their activities in relation to the world in which they live. Whether the events composing the pattern are true or false, objectively considered, need not concern him. [2]

[1] Page 134 of this volume.   [2] Page 76 of this volume.

At this point Becker's conception of history and of the historian's work made contact with philosophy. His fundamental idea was one often explored by philosophers after Kant (and no doubt to be found before him), that it is the specific property of mind or consciousness to span time and thus to draw together, or to focus in the present, an experience which carries its past and which is continually redirected toward an expanding future. In his own day Becker found this philosophical idea most congenially expressed in the psychology and the pragmatism of William James. Mind is thus a union of memory, which binds man to what he has done, and of intelligence, which restates and reconstructs the past suitably to the present and in the prospect of what he hopes to do in the future. Since this is essentially the nature of mind, it is also essentially the nature of human society, or of the culture upon which a human society is built. From this point of view there can be no radical separation of intelligence from feeling and purpose, or of mind from behavior and action. For intelligence is a capacity to use the means at hand for a purpose, to adapt old ideas to new situations, to solve the problems set by an ever changing environment, and to enable conduct to deal effectively with a future which can be neither arrested nor stereotyped. Its work is perennially destructive and constructive: destructive because it must restate the formulas of a past that has become outmoded; constructive because it must seek restated formulas adequate to the purposes and aspirations of the future. Thought, whether in the individual or the race, is continuous, but it is never unchanging.

This philosophical idea, which Becker saw gaining cur-

rency in liberal American thought at the turn of the century, was congenial to his own temperament, which also was notably liberal and enlightened but temperate, ironic, and skeptical of unconditional commitments. He saw in it a formula for what interested him most in intellectual history and also a clue to the historian's role in society. Every historical period, he believed, has its characteristic intellectual style—its "climate of opinion," as he came to call it—a constellation of related ideas largely inherited but constantly undergoing change under the impact of new conditions which set new problems and demand new solutions. Its history is at bottom the story of these adaptations and a description of the conditions that occasioned them. This conception largely accounts for those periods and phases of modern history that Becker found most interesting. These were, first, the democratic ideas of the eighteenth-century Enlightenment, which had to be continually expanded and modified as they traveled westward in the wake of the American frontier, and, second, the ideas of the Enlightenment itself as they took form in the transition from the Christian Middle Ages under the impact of modern science and technology. The historian, moreover, plays a significant part in this process of revision and reconstruction, for his account of the past is indispensable in clarifying present purpose and intelligent achievement. Ingrained in his character and essential to his work there must be a *concern,* a deep involvement with the fate of the movements, the ideas, and the institutions that he recounts. This belief underlies Becker's criticism of what was called in his day "scientific" history, exemplified in this collection by the essays entitled "Detachment and the Writing of History" and

"What Are Historical Facts?" The notion that history could be written merely by recounting facts seemed to Becker flatly impossible, and the notion that the historian's detachment could be identified with indifference seemed to him an invitation to triviality. For facts require interpretation, and interpretation depends at the very least on selection, and selection can be made only in the light of meaning, significance, or the bearing of fact on some object of human interest.

Much that Becker had to say on the method of history, like the philosophy to which it was related, is now in a sense dated. In truth it united two positions that are logically independent if not incoherent. His emphasis on what he called "relativism" seemed to imply the dissolution of all "absolute" ends or values which might define the direction of social progress, and repeatedly he used language which suggested that this was indeed his meaning. Yet his profoundest moral convictions were all on the side of a belief that some ideals—specifically those embodied in the democratic liberties—were in substance unchangeable and were indispensable, at least in a civilized human society. These the Enlightenment had conceived as self-evident moral truths, yet there is no apparent reason why historical continuity of itself must move toward the realization or even the preservation of these values. In the light of historical relativism there seemed no reason why democracy should be construed as more than a generous but otherwise unfounded optimism. The success of dictatorship first in Italy and then in Germany and Russia had a powerful impact on Becker's later writings. These are in substance the reaffirmation of a faith, eloquently expressed and quite in accord with

what Becker had always believed, but without much logical dependence on his philosophy of historical writing.

Yet this affirmation of faith may prove to be the abiding element in Becker's writing of history. For it united
values which he attributed to democracy with values
which, as he said,

are older and more universal than democracy and do not
depend upon it. They have a life of their own apart from any
particular social system or type of civilization. They are the
values which, since the time of Buddha and Confucius, Solo-
mon and Zoroaster, Plato and Aristotle, Socrates and Jesus,
men have commonly employed to measure the advance or the
decline of civilization, the values they have celebrated in the
saints and sages whom they have agreed to canonize.[3]

It was this belief in the ethical continuity of all the
higher civilizations that underlay Becker's conviction of
the moral seriousness of the historian's calling and of the
importance of history as a factor, at once intellectual and
artistically imaginative, in the life of society. The historian, as Becker conceived him, is a man set apart by a
kind of social division of labor to do, in the broadest perspective possible and with the highest professional standards of intelligence and integrity, what every man must
do by the rough-and-ready standards of everyday life. The
history that he writes is an agency by which his society is
enabled to understand what it is doing, in the light of
what it has done and of what it hopes to do. It is a joint
product—as Becker believed all significant science and
art to be—of freedom and responsibility: freedom to inquire and to follow wherever rational argument may

[3] *New Liberties for Old* (New Haven, 1941), pp. 149–150.

lead; responsibility in the use of freedom and in applying the results of inquiry. In the end it presumes some intrinsic union of intelligence, integrity, and good will.

I believe, without being able to prove but equally without being able to doubt, that the primary values of life, upon which in the long run all other values depend, are intelligence, integrity, and good will. Taken separately, any one of these may avail little. Good will, apart from intelligence and integrity, may be a futile or even a vicious thing. Intelligence leads to knowledge, and knowledge confers power, enabling men to transform instead of endlessly to repeat their activities. But knowledge and the power it confers may be used either to degrade or to ennoble the life of man. Only when guided and restrained by good will and integrity can they be used effectively to achieve the good life.[4]

Thus Becker's thought closed with a question rather than an answer, the question of morals in a world of power, to which the generation following Becker also has no answer.

GEORGE H. SABINE

Ithaca, New York
May 9, 1958

---

[4] *Ibid.,* pp. xvi–xvii.

I

ON HISTORY

Detachment and the
Writing of History

THE witty remark of Dumas, that Lamartine had raised
history to the dignity of romance, would have appealed to
Thomas Buckle, who was much occupied with reducing
it to the level of a science. Critics have told us that the
attempt of the latter was a flat failure. But the attitude of
the critics toward Buckle is less reassuring than the attitude of the scientists toward history; for while the former
maintain that Buckle pursued a good end by a false
method, the latter to this day reproach history with being entertaining and useless.*

The remarks of Herbert Spencer in this connection
are well known to every one. But perhaps there are some
who have not heard the complaint of Professor Minot,
who recently took occasion, in some public addresses, to
lament the quite obvious futility of present historical
methods. Whereas, in all other departments of knowledge
great and useful advances were being made, historians

* An essay first published in *The Atlantic Monthly,* CVI (Oct.
1910), 524–536; reprinted by permission of *The Atlantic Monthly.*

3

alone were industriously engaged in aimless endeavor. In this opinion he had been confirmed only the summer before, when he had carried with him to the mountains, or wherever it was that he spent his vacation, a work which he supposed represented the best that modern historical scholarship could offer—the first volume of the *Cambridge Modern History!* A part of his summer had been pleasantly spent in perusing this work. In it he found much of interest: events related in great detail; facts, curious and suggestive, presented, the truth of which could doubtless not be questioned. But of fruitful generalization, there was little indeed, no effort having been made, apparently, to reduce the immense mass of facts to principles of universal validity.

I do not suppose there are many historians who carry the *Cambridge Modern History* with them to the mountains. It is not a book to be read in the greenwood. Certainly, the vision of the eminent professor dropping the ponderous tome into a vacation trunk, and pressing the lid deliberately down without a qualm, is pathetic enough. And yet the *Cambridge Modern History* is a serious work. If it is not the best that modern historical scholarship can do, it should be. Until Professor Minot found it interesting, no one, I imagine, ever thought it in danger of being classed as literature. If it is not science, it is nothing.

Professor Minot, who is perfectly clear about its not being science, in spite of its being entertaining, would doubtless find the lively remarks of Bagehot, in his essay on Gibbon, even more entertaining.

Whatever may be the uses of this sort of composition in itself and abstractly, it is certainly of great use relatively and

to literary men. Consider the position of a man of that
species. He sits beside a library fire, with nice white paper,
a good pen, a capital style, every means of saying everything,
but nothing to say; of course he is an able man,—but still
one cannot always have original ideas. Every day cannot be
an era,—and how dull it is to make it your business to
write, to stay by yourself in a room to write, and then to
have nothing to say! What a gain if something would happen! Then one could describe it. Something has happened,
and that something is history. Perhaps when a Visigoth broke
a head, he thought that that was all. Not so: he was making
history; Gibbon has written it down.

Humorous sallies like this are to be enjoyed, but happily need not be answered. At least it is so in this case,
for most historians will readily agree with Professor Minot
that the *Cambridge Modern History* contains a great mass
of facts the truth of which cannot be questioned. But they
will think that in saying so he has given the book a very
good character indeed. You cannot disconcert the orthodox historian of our day by saying that he has got a mass
of facts together without knowing what to do with them:
if the truth of them cannot indeed be questioned, he will
know very well what to do with them: he will put them
in a book. But imagine the sentiments of the authors if
Professor Minot had said that "the beautifully coördi-
nated generalizations, with which the *Cambridge Modern
History* is packed, are most stimulating and suggestive."
Their chagrin would have been immense! No, the modern
historian is not given to generalization. It is not his
business to generalize,—so, at least, he thinks; it is his
business to find out and to record "exactly what hap-

pened." So far, Bagehot is quite right after all. History is
what happened; the historian must write it down, if not
like Gibbon, at least *wie es ist eigentlich gewesen.*

If historians take this attitude somewhat uncompro-
misingly, it is not because they do not care for scientific
history. Quite the contrary! They care for nothing so
much; and to contribute a little to such history—to make
"a permanent contribution to knowledge"—is their chief-
est ambition. Yet the thoughtful man knows well, in spite
of what the reviewers say every month, that it is not easy to
make a permanent contribution to knowledge. In nearly
every age, able men have written histories; of them all, a
few have proved permanent contributions to literature;
as history, not one but must be edited. Even the great
masters, whom we loyally advise every one to read without
reading ourselves, do not escape. Of course Tacitus was
a great writer, but he was not at all scientific: he had ideas,
and they were, unfortunately, the ideas of a Roman republican. Even Gibbon, with all his fine lack of enthusiasm, gave expression to the eighteenth-century dream
of a golden age. Finding nothing in the Middle Ages but
the "triumph of barbarism and Christianity," he too, in
his ponderous fashion, voiced the demand *écraser l'infâme!*

As for the favorite historians of the nineteenth century,
a decade or a generation has sufficed in most cases to shelve
their works behind glass doors, now rarely opened. Ceas-
ing to be read, they are advertised as standard by publishers, and fall at last to be objects of glib criticism by
the young professor who has himself written a monograph
and three book-reviews. Not a life of drudgery, or genius
itself, shall avoid disaster. Faith in democracy discredits
a history of Greece; lack of it inspires the apotheosis

of Caesar. Hatred of tractarianism guides a facile pen through twelve volumes. The Reform Bill is read back into the Revolution of 1688. The memory of Sedan becomes a misleading gloss in all Merovingian manuscripts. Little wonder if the modern historian, stumbling over the wreckage that strews his path, has no desire to add anything of his own to the débris. Much better, he thinks, to be employed quarrying out of the bedrock of historical fact even one stone, so it be chiseled four-square, that may find its niche in the permanent structure of some future master-builder.

This attitude of mind is not peculiar to historians. In every field of intellectual activity, men of science are reconstructing the cosmos in terms of the evolutionary hypothesis. We are most of us quite proud of having reduced the universe to unstable equilibrium, and yet there is one thing that seems to be exempt from the operation of this law of change and adaptation which incessantly transforms everything else—truth itself: everything is unstable except the idea of instability. It is true, the Pragmatists are asking whether, if everything ' .abject to the law of change, truth be not subject to the law of change, and reality as well—the very facts themselves. But whatever scientists may think of this notion, historians have not yet been disturbed by it. For them, certainly, truth is a fixed quality: the historical reality, the "fact," is a thing purely objective, that does not change; a thing, therefore, that can be established once for all beyond any peradventure. So well established is this idea, that it has been formulated in a law of history.

Il y a toujours un correspondance entre les faits intellectuels, et l'état général des esprits; une loi qui a comme corollaire

la suivante: le changement du milieu intellectuel entraine toujours un changement dans les faits de l'esprit qu'il entoure. La vérité seule n'est pas soumise à l'influence du milieu; elle ne change pas avec le dernier.[1]

The truth, which alone changes not, is what must be got at. The objective reality must be caught, as it were, and mounted like a specimen for the instruction of future ages. But this is exceedingly difficult, precisely because "le changement du milieu intellectuel entraine toujours un changement dans les faits de l'esprit qu'il entoure." This difficulty must therefore be the rock on which all previous historians have split. Not sufficiently aware of the disastrous influence of the *milieu,* they have unconsciously read the objective facts of the past in the light of their own purposes, or the preoccupations of their own age.

But, after all, how is it possible to avoid the influence of one's *milieu?* No one has given any very precise answer to this question, but there is a favorite phrase, familiar to every seminary fledgeling, that is supposed to point the way: one must cultivate complete *mental detachment.* Those who seek truth, says Renan, must have "no mental reservations referring to human affairs," must "beware of every formula which may one day become an obstacle to the free development of their minds"; as for histories, they should be written "with as much supreme indifference as if they were written in another planet." But it is Nietzsche who has sketched for us, in his inimitable manner, the portrait of the detached man:—

The objective man is in truth a mirror: accustomed to prostration before everything that wants to be known, with

---

[1] Xenopol, *Les Principes fondamentaux de l'histoire,* p. 197.

such desires only as knowing or "reflecting" imply—he waits until something comes, and then expands himself sensitively, so that even the light footsteps and gliding past of spiritual beings may not be lost on his surface and film. Whatever "personality" he still possesses seems to him . . . disturbing; so much has he come to regard himself as the passage and reflection of outside forms and events. . . . Should one wish love or hatred from him . . . he will do what he can, and furnish what he can. But one must not be surprised if it should not be much. . . . His mirroring and eternally self-polishing soul no longer knows how to affirm, no longer how to deny; he does not command; neither does he destroy. . . . Neither is he a model man; he does not go in advance of any one, nor after either; he places himself generally too far off to have any reason for espousing the cause of either good or evil. . . . He is an instrument . . . but nothing in himself—*presque rien!* [2]

This is surely M. Renan's man of "supreme indifference." If you like, you may believe there never was such a man: the wonderful creature is doubtless only an ideal. The ideal, nevertheless, is clear enough. It is an ideal based upon the familiar conception of the "pure reason" —reason cut loose from will and emotion, from purpose and passion and desire, all these left behind, or nonexistent, burned away perhaps with some methodological purifying flame. Intelligence, thus reduced to a kind of delicate mechanical instrument, set carefully in a sealed case to protect it from deflecting influences of environment, we are to suppose capable of acting automatically when brought in contact with objective phenomena. These phenomena—the "facts" of history, for example —come before it, "wanting to be known"; it expands

[2] *Beyond Good and Evil,* p. 140.

itself sensitively, and truth is registered upon its polished surface, as objects are upon a photographic plate. Only in this manner can we know the thing *wie es ist eigentlich gewesen;* but in this manner, if at all, we shall surely be able to record exactly what happened.

Certainly there is something impressive in the assertion that it is the business of the historian to "get the facts." In our generation, the mere word "fact" is something to conjure with. Your practical friend, in some discussion or other, ends by saying roundly, "But it is not a question of theory; it is a question of fact."

Of course you give it up. A fact is something substantial, something material, something you can perhaps take up in your hand, or stand upon: it will always bear your weight. And so, with much talk about "cold facts," and "hard facts," and not being able to "get around the facts," it has come to a pass where the historical fact seems almost material too, something that can be handed about and pressed with the thumb to test its solidity. But, in truth, the historical fact is a thing wonderfully elusive after all, very difficult to fix, almost impossible to distinguish from "theory," to which it is commonly supposed to be so completely antithetical.

It is said to be a fact that Caesar was stabbed by the senators, in the senate-house at Rome; and this is, I suppose, as simple a fact as one will ordinarily deal with: as hard as any, and quite as difficult to get around, if one should wish, for some sinister purpose, to get around it. But it is really simple only in the sense that it is a simple statement easily comprehended. It is itself made up of many simpler facts: the senators standing round, the words that were said, the scuffle, the three and twenty

dagger-strokes,—numberless facts, indeed, make the single fact that Caesar was stabbed in the senate-house.

With equal facility, this single fact may be combined with others to form a more complex, but still relatively simple fact,—the fact that Antony, Octavius, and Lepidus replaced Caesar in the government of Rome. Thus, while we speak of historical facts as if they were pebbles to be gathered in a cup, there is in truth no unit fact in history. The historical reality is continuous, and infinitely complex; and the cold hard facts into which it is said to be analyzed are not concrete portions of the reality, but only aspects of it. The reality of history has forever disappeared, and the "facts" of history, whatever they once were, are only mental images or pictures which the historian makes in order to comprehend it.

How, then, are these images formed? Not from the reality directly, for the reality has ceased to exist. But the reality has left certain traces, and these help us to construct the image. Some one saw Caesar stabbed, and afterwards wrote down, let us suppose, this:—

On the Ides of March, Caesar was stabbed by the senators in the senate-house at the base of Pompey's statue, which all the while ran blood.

I suppose myself an historian, reading this statement. As I read, a mental picture is at once formed: several men in a room, at the base of a statue, driving daggers into one of their number. But it is not the statement alone that enables me to form the picture: my own experience enters in. I have seen men and rooms and daggers, and my experience of these things furnishes the elements of which the picture is composed. Suppose me to know

nothing of the ancient Roman world: my picture would doubtless be composed of the senate-chamber at Washington, of men in frock coats, and of bowie-knives, perhaps. It is true, the picture changes as I read more of the Roman world. Yet at each step in this transformation, it is still my own experience that furnishes the new elements for the new picture. New sources enable me to combine the elements of experience more correctly, but experience must furnish the elements to select from. The "facts" of history do not exist for any historian until he creates them, and into every fact that he creates some part of his individual experience must enter.

But experience not only furnishes the elements for the image which the sources guide us in forming: it is also the final court of appeal in evaluating the sources themselves. History rests on testimony, but the qualitative value of testimony is determined in the last analysis by tested and accepted experience. The historian, no less than the scientist, smiles at the naïveté of Joseph de Maistre, who imagined that the negations of science could be destroyed by the assertions of history. With a single perfectly proved historical fact, he courageously proposed to defy the whole tribe of geometers,—"J'ai à vous répondre qu'Archimède brûle la flotte romaine avec un miroir ardent,"—if it were once perfectly proved.

But the historian knows well that no amount of testimony is ever permitted to establish as past reality a thing that cannot be found in present reality. And it is not enough to be able to find in present experience the elements for a picture of the alleged past fact. One can, for example, readily picture the destruction of the Roman fleet by means of a burning-glass, or the bleeding of

Pompey's statue; the elements for such pictures are familiar. But the sources ask us to make a combination of the elements which the registered experience of our age does not warrant. In every other case the witness may have a perfect character—all that goes for nothing. Tacitus is a good witness, and when he says the Germans do not inhabit cities, we believe him, though we do not know precisely what he means by cities. But when he says that Tiberius, having lived for fifty years a sane and well-ordered life, became quite suddenly a monster of lust and cruelty, we do not believe him so readily. If he had said a thousand times over that the Germans had wings, we should still say that the Germans had no wings.

The classic expression of this truth is of course Hume's famous argument against miracles. That argument does not really prove that miracles never occurred in history; it proves only that there is no use having a past through which the intellect cannot freely range with a certain sense of security. If we cannot be on familiar terms with our past, it is no good. We must have a past that is the product of all the present. With sources that say it was not so, we will have nothing to do; better still, we will make them say it was so. The sources say—and it is a commonplace now that they say nothing more persistently, or with greater particularization of detail—that during the Middle Ages miracles were as common as lies. The modern historian admits that there were lies, but denies that there were miracles. He not only rejects the miracle,—the explanation of the fact,—he rejects the facts as well; he says that such facts are not proved; for him, there were no such facts. And he rejects these facts, not because they are contrary to every possible law of

nature, to every possible experience, but simply because they are contrary to the comparatively few laws of nature which his generation is willing to regard as established. But as rapidly as scientists can find a place for such facts in experience, historians will create them in history,—a truth which the progress of psychical research promises to illustrate in a striking manner. Even now, indeed, Anatole France and Andrew Lang cannot agree about certain facts of the fifteenth century, because one of them takes psychical research seriously, while the other thinks it is all moonshine.

If the reality of history can be reached only through the door of present experience, one may well ask how our objective man, so detached and indifferent, with no mental reservations referring to human affairs, will proceed in determining the facts. There he sits in Mars,—or, better still, the British Museum,—ready to expand sensitively when something comes, wanting to be known. Unfortunately, nothing comes. Our perfectly detached man is mildly distressed, perhaps, to find that the thing first of all absolutely required is an act of will: a painful thing, and, strictly speaking, impossible for him. Suppose this difficult step once taken, still there is nothing before him but paper with writing on it; and I think he may expand himself sensitively for an endless term with no great result. The trouble is that the dead manuscripts do not "want to be known"; about that, they are as detached as can be. Our objective man must himself want to know, and wanting to know implies a purpose in knowing. Even the will to be purely objective is itself a purpose, becoming not infrequently a passion, creating the facts in its own image.

But we are not told that the business of the historian is limited to finding out exactly what happened; he must also record exactly what happened. It is the fashion to call this the problem of synthesis, as distinguished from investigation, criticism, or analysis. The distinction is doubtless a convenient one, but it will not bear too close inspection. If there is no unit fact in history, if the facts are only mental images, why, then, it must be very difficult to assert a fact without thereby making a synthesis. "Caesar was stabbed in the senate-house" is a fact, but it is also a synthesis of other facts. Strictly speaking, analysis and synthesis cannot be rigidly distinguished. And the reason is not far to seek: it is because there is no real analysis and no real synthesis. When the historian is engaged in what the methodologists call analysis, it is not the reality that he takes apart, but only the sources,—a very different matter.

Perfect analysis is achieved when each source is transformed into as many statements as it explicitly or implicitly contains. These statements are then set down on separate cards or slips of paper; and with these cards the historian must be content, for the simple reason that nothing better is possible. Even this analysis is, indeed, not always possible. For some periods of history it is possible, but for most of modern history, at least, it remains only an ideal: a wilderness of slips would not suffice for even a few years; so that, if scientific history is inseparable from complete analysis of the sources, we are confronted with the disquieting paradox that the less knowledge we have of history the more scientific that knowledge becomes.

Without attempting to resolve this difficulty, let us

suppose the work of analysis already finished: all the
sources critically edited, separated into their simplest
statements, recorded on separate cards ticketed with date
and reference, arranged chronologically. There are the
"facts"; it remains to construct the synthesis. The chrono-
logical arrangement would, sure enough, be no mean
synthesis in itself. One may ask what, after all, remains
to be done by our objective man, sitting there before
his card-cases, intent to record exactly what happened.
Everything that happened, so far as any trace of it is left,
is already recorded, it seems. But the truth is, no one is
satisfied with that, unless it be our objective man. For
most of us, afflicted with mere human purposes, a case
full of cards may be magnificent, but it is not history.
Out of these cards we *will* get some useful, intelligible
meaning. The problem of synthesis is, indeed, not to
record exactly what happened, but by simplification to
convey an intelligible meaning of what happened. With
that problem every constructive historian is engaged from
the first step to the last.

This necessary simplification may be achieved, I suppose, in one of two ways: by classification in terms of
common qualities, or by grouping in terms of concrete
relations. Comparing what is related of all kings (assuming that the term king is precisely understood), the
historian may find that all kings have been crowned.
This quality common to all kings is then reduced to a
single statement, "all kings are crowned." This is the
method of the natural sciences, and of sociology as well.
Certainly, it is a method well worth while; but, as we
are all agreed that history is not sociology, it cannot be
the method of the historian. The historian, therefore,

proceeds by the other method. Concerned with a particular king, he will group the facts related of this particular king, according to their concrete relations, thus:—

George III, having succeeded to the throne of England October 25, 1760, was immediately proclaimed in the customary manner, and formally crowned at Westminster, September 22, 1761.

The historian, like the sociologist, has simplified the facts for the purpose of conveying an intelligible meaning. But the difference between the two methods is profound. The statement that all kings are crowned is an abstraction, a generalization of qualities common to all kings. From this generalization, it can be inferred of any actual king that he was crowned, and that inference every one must make, because the statement implies just that and nothing else. But the statement about George III is not an abstraction. It is just as concrete as any of the numberless particular statements upon which it is based. From it no particular fact can be deduced: it cannot be inferred that the Privy Council met, or that mounted heralds went forth reading a solemn document on the London streets to crowds of gaping people. The historian knows that these things were done, and he has crowded them all into the term "proclaimed." But for the reader, unless he already knows that kings in England were customarily proclaimed in that way, the term will have only a vague significance: something was done, he does not know what.

The sociologist has simplified by combining particular facts in a generalization, from which any one can deduce

again the particular fact, and no other. The historian has simplified by selecting, from a number of particular facts, certain facts which he considers most important to be known.

It seems, then, that the great point in historical synthesis is selection: which of the numberless particular facts shall the historian select? One wishes to know at once, therefore, if there is some objective standard for determining the relative value of facts; a standard which, being applied by any number of trained historians, will give the same result in each case. Well, yes, we are told there is such a standard, and one residing in the facts themselves, and therefore purely objective. The facts to be selected for constructing what is called the "historical concept" have four chief characteristics which, for the initiated, distinguish them as clearly as if they were labeled "for historians only."

Professor Fling, in his admirable summary of the elaborate work of Rickert,[3] tells us what these characteristics are: the historian selects facts that are unique, facts that have value on account of their uniqueness, facts that are causally connected, facts that reveal unique change or evolution. Historians who proceed thus, proceed scientifically; and while it is doubtless true that no two historians will use identical terms in phrasing their "concepts," yet "the progress of historical synthesis means a growing agreement among scientific historians touching the important facts of this or that period." "If they pro-

---

[3] *American Historical Review,* vol. ix, p. 1. I am aware, of course, that the views I am criticizing are not necessarily those of Professor Fling, since he has done no more than to present, for American readers, the theories of Rickert.

ceed scientifically," the same facts will be selected "by the opponents of the French Revolution . . . as have been selected by the supporters of it." It seems, therefore, if this is indeed a practical standard for evaluating the facts of history, and one truly objective, that we have at last a kind of philosophical recipe for making our contributions permanent; a guide sufficient even for one who has attained complete detachment, or for our disinterested objective man. One has only to examine the facts, select such as bear the mark, and put them together: the result is sure.

Nevertheless, the use of the word value in this formula is disquieting. The difficulties which it is sure to raise have been recognized, but not altogether disposed of. "The use of the word value," says Professor Fling, "seems to introduce an uncertain and arbitrary element into the problem. But the question of value is not a question of partisanship, nor of approval or disapproval; it is a question of importance. Is this fact important for the Reformation? Is an account of the Reformation intelligible without it? The Protestant may love Luther, the Catholic may hate him, but they would agree that Luther is important for the Reformation."

To say that the question of value is a question of importance, does little to resolve the difficulty. We still ask, Important for what? The answer is, Important for the Reformation. But I suppose the Reformation is one of those very "concepts" which Professor Fling is telling us how to construct in a scientific manner. All that we yet know, therefore, is that the concept is formed by selecting the facts that are important for the concept. If Protestant and Catholic have a concept of the Reformation to begin

with, the concept is not determined by the facts; if they have no concept to begin with, why is Luther more important than Tetzel? Indeed, the historian may be neither Protestant nor Catholic, and to him I should think the Reformation might be perfectly intelligible if Luther's part in it were reduced to very slight proportions; to him, it might be intelligible on that ground only. Have we not already been told that the Reformation was primarily an illustration, on a grand scale, of the law of diminishing returns? That concept, if it is intelligible at all, is intelligible without Luther.

After all, do the facts come first and determine the concept, or does the concept come first and determine the facts? The heart of the question is there. It seems that Professor Fling virtually admits that the concept comes first.

The historical method is thus teleological in a certain sense. The subject of an historical investigation is a unique thing. . . . It has beginning and end. We know what the end was, and we wish to know what the chain of events was that led up to the final event. We seek such facts, to be wrought up into a synthesis, as may be necessary to show how the end was attained.

We know what the end was. But in what sense do we know what the end was, of the French Revolution, for example? Of the French Revolution, surely the end is not yet. Lord Morley tells us that it is still some way from being fully accomplished.

The process is still going on, and a man of M. Taine's lively intellectual sensibility can no more escape its influence than he can escape the ingredients of the air he breathes.

And if we hold to the doctrine of the continuity of history, how far back must we go to find a period that is fully accomplished? In truth, we know the end only in part. The historians may choose to consider the Restoration of 1815 as the end of the French Revolution; but his concept of that end, which must determine the facts he selects, will be born of the age in which he lives. One can scarcely imagine any historian living in 1825, even the most scientific in the world, having the same concept of the Restoration that Professor Fling has. Unfortunately, the historian and his concepts are a part of the very process he would interpret; the end of that process is ever changing, and the historian will scarcely avoid changing with it, whether he have the lively intellectual sensibility of M. Taine, or be as placid as Nietzsche's objective man.

If the historian could indeed separate himself from the process which he describes, if he were outside of history as the chemist is outside of chemistry, his greatest success should be with those periods that differ most from the one in which he lives. But he has, in fact, most success with those periods in which men's habitual modes of thought and action most resemble his own. Strange and remote events, to be synthesized intelligibly at all, must be interpreted in terms of motives that are familiar. It is true, the actions of men in all past ages have been such as to justify us in assuming a fundamental similarity in human motives. Yet familiar motives are much more intensely felt in some ages than in others.

The religious motive is still active in the twentieth century, but the exaggerated asceticism of the Middle Ages already partakes of the unreal. The historian finds

that for some centuries men entered monasteries and lived impossible lives of self-stultification, and they did this, so the documents tell him, for the love of God and the salvation of souls. But the love of God, expressing itself in that fashion, is remote from us of the twentieth century. It no longer satisfies us to label monasteries with the words "salvation of souls," and so we are writing over their portals the words "economic institutions" instead. Did they not serve as inns, and recover much marsh land? Of this exaggerated asceticism, St. Simeon Stylites is the classic example. In explaining him, the modern historian, whether M. Taine or another, has some difficulty. Not that he finds it impossible to form an image of the poor monk standing there; he can form the image perfectly. Nor can he reject the fact because contrary to observed experience; he has seen men standing at the top of a pillar, has done it himself, or could do it, perhaps. To find a motive that would induce him to do what Stylites is said to have done,—the difficulty is there. He can't just explain him by the lack of inns. So he says, "interesting pathological case," and passes quickly on. Stylites is really too remote.

For the normal child, St. Simeon would be perhaps one of the least remote objects of the whole Middle Ages, because the child, even the twentieth-century child, lives in a world which we do not know, and which we are therefore pleased to call the world of fancy. The child is, in fact, perfectly detached from all those dull practical interests with which mature men are so preoccupied. He is as indifferent to them as if he did indeed live in another planet; and yet he makes a synthesis of the historical reality that would fail to satisfy, I suppose, even M.

Renan. A fairly obedient child, it is true, will make any synthesis you require of him; but he regards it, for the most part, as a meaningless and vexatious business. For him, the reality is whatever relates itself to his interests, whatever co-ordinates readily with his dream world. He is unpatriotic enough to prefer the winged gods of Greece to John Smith or Daniel Boone. Seven-league boots and one-eyed men, impossible ladies and knight-errant without purpose, St. Simeon Stylites standing, solemn and useless, at the top of a pillar,—from these he is not detached. He, too, has a concept of the end, and will, if left to himself, select the facts that are important for that concept, thereby constructing a synthesis quite true and valuable for his purposes.

The method of the trained historian is not essentially different, I suspect, from that of the child. He achieves a different result, it is true; but that is because he has a different "concept" round which to group the facts—a concept derived from the practical or intellectual interests that concern him. If there is a "growing agreement among scientific historians touching the important facts of this or that period," it is because there is, in every age, a certain response in the world of thought to dominant social forces. But the agreement is only for the particular age; the next age, or the next generation, will think very differently. In an age of political revolution there is perhaps a growing agreement that "history is past politics." In an age when industrial problems are pressing for solution the "economic interpretation of history" is the thing. The advent of the social state will doubtless give us some new formula. Whatever it may be, the historian of the future will select the facts that are important for

that concept. The historian, as Professor Fling has said, does indeed have a concept of the end, and he selects the facts that will explain how that end came about. But it is the concept that determines the facts, not the facts the concept.

From beginning to end, the historian is outside the subject of his investigation,—"the life of an historical personage, a battle, an economic crisis, a period in the life of a people," or whatever it is that he professes to confine himself to. Instead of "sticking to the facts," the facts stick to him, if he has any ideas to attract them; and they will stick to him to some purpose only if his ideas are many, vivid, and fruitful. Complete detachment would produce few histories, and none worth while; for the really detached mind is a dead mind, lying among the facts of history like unmagnetized steel among iron-filings, no synthesis ever resulting, in one case or the other, to the end of time.

Consider the trained historian, intent on studying the sixteenth century. Before him are the analyzed sources —the "facts"—neatly arranged in cases. He begins thumbing the cards, reading the statements, taking in the facts. Doubtless he says to himself:—

This fact is unique, important because unique, causally connected; I will therefore set it aside to be wrought up into my final synthesis.

No such thing. As he goes over and over his cards, some aspects of the reality recorded there interest him more, others less; some are retained, others forgotten; some have power to start a new train of thought; some appear to be causally connected; some logically connected; some are

without perceptible connection of any sort. And the reason is simple: some facts strike the mind as interesting or suggestive, have a meaning of some sort, lead to some desirable end, because they associate themselves with ideas already in the mind; they fit in somehow to the ordered experience of the historian. This original synthesis—not to be confused with the making of a book for the printer, a very different matter—is only half deliberate. It is accomplished almost automatically. The mind *will* select and discriminate from the very beginning. It is the whole "apperceiving mass" that does the business, seizing upon this or that new impression and building it into its own growing content. As new facts are taken in, the old ideas or concepts, it is true, are modified, distinguished, destroyed even; but the modified ideas become new centres of attraction. And so the process is continued, for years it may be. The final synthesis is doubtless composed of facts unique, causally connected, revealing unique change; but the unique fact, selected because of its importance, was in every case selected because of its importance for some idea already in possession of the field. The original concepts, which give character to the entire synthesis, were contributed, not by the facts of the sixteenth century, but by the facts of the twentieth century.

If the modern historian exhibits detachment, certainly it is not from the dominant ideas of his own age. The very purpose of the age is to comprehend without purpose, to judge of the event by the event itself, to register a fact and call it a law. The effort to be purely objective, the aversion from stereotyped religious and political formulae, the solemn determination to see the thing as it

really is,—these are fixed concepts, round which the historian constructs his synthesis. It is not because he is detached from his environment, but because he is pre-occupied with a certain phase of it, that his history becomes "scientific"—something more than a chronicle, something less than literature. The modern historian, for example, is detached from any fixed idea in religion, placing himself "too far off—for espousing the cause of either good or evil." But he knows well that he must espouse, with fine enthusiasm, the cause of not espousing any cause. His synthesis must vindicate, not Luther or Leo X, but his own ideal of detachment. Was Catholicism or Protestantism true, or good, or useful? Why, both and neither, cries the modern historian, and he can answer you that without ever having expanded himself sensitively before the one or the other. In so far as either existed, it was necessary, adapted to the conditions, and therefore doubtless good and true. Whatever happens, the historian will be detached; he will not take sides.

But it is difficult not to take sides if sharp contrasts and impassable gulfs are permitted to appear. If one could serve neither God nor Mammon, it is necessary to dispense with both. The modern historian has therefore a concept, a preconcept, of continuity and evolution, with "natural law" at the back of things. The historical reality must be conceived as all of a piece, like a woven garment. In things evil must be perceived an element of things good, and in things good an element of things evil. Facts which do not contribute to establish these concepts will not be selected; they may be unique, but they are judged not important. No man is a hero to his valet. Doubtless valets have a definite concept of what masters are, and select only the facts that are important for that

concept. Nowadays, certainly, no man is a hero to his biographer, much less a villain. The historical mind is detached from all concepts of that sort, and thus Napoleon becomes a necessary process instead of a scoundrel. Do you ask the modern historian whether he loves Luther or hates him? What a question! It is not to Luther, but to the Law of Diminishing Returns, that we owe religious liberty.

There is profound truth in the biting remark of Voltaire, that, after all, history is only a pack of tricks we play on the dead. If useful social ends are served, it does not harm the dead, who had in any case tricks of their own. The trick of every past age—of St. Augustine, of Bossuet, of Gibbon and Rousseau and Voltaire himself, all the brilliant legerdemain of the eighteenth century—has long since been exposed. Yet it is the theory of the detached historian himself that these syntheses served, like every vital institution, a certain social purpose. If the medieval Church was necessary to preserve Europe from anarchy, a synthesis like St. Augustine's, creating history in the image of the Church, was surely necessary and useful. If "enlightenment" was all that could save Europe from obscurantism in the eighteenth century, a synthesis of history proving the Church indispensable to human welfare, as the modern synthesis does, would have been beside the mark, quite useless, and impossible. And so the synthesis constructed by modern historians may very likely have its uses. When old landmarks are being washed away, and old foundations are crumbling to dust, it is doubtless useful and necessary to conceive the historical reality as continuous, causally connected, and changing only in response to forces largely remote from purposive human will.

Some future Lord Morley will tell the world how the histories of the nineteenth century served a useful social purpose, and did "a certain amount of good in a bad way." And if useful and necessary, then true—true in the only way that historical synthesis is ever likely to be true, true relatively to the needs of the age which fashioned it. At least, it is difficult to understand how the modern man, so wedded to the doctrine of evolution, can conceive of historical synthesis as true in any absolute sense. Institutions, he would agree, are true or false only as they are adapted for survival. But there is, is there not, an evolution of ideas too, only the fittest surviving? One can readily imagine the doctrine of survival of the fittest proving socially disintegrating in the end, in which case some other hypothesis will doubtless prove itself fittest to survive by surviving in fact.

Certainly, the evolutionary hypothesis gives us no assurance that detachment will forever be in fashion among historians. The state of mind best calculated to find out exactly what happened is perhaps incompatible with a disposition to care greatly what it is that happened; and whatever value the notion of detachment may have just now, the time may come—there have been such times in the past—when it is more important that every one should care greatly what happens. In that case, one can hardly think of the "objective man" as possessing qualities exceptionally well adapted for survival. Then we may perhaps have histories as interesting as Professor Minot imagines the *Cambridge Modern History* is now. One scarcely ventures to hope they will be as scientific as he thinks they ought to be.

Review of Henry Adams'
The Degradation of the Democratic Dogma

THE reader will not find anything in this volume from the pen of Henry Adams bearing the title "The Degradation of the Democratic Dogma." He will find the brief letter to H. B. Adams, written in December, 1894, to serve in lieu of a presidential address before the American Historical Association, already published in the *Reports* of the Association; the *Letter to American Teachers of History,* privately printed in 1910; and an essay entitled "The Rule of Phase Applied to History," now printed for the first time. These three papers, together making 186 pages possess a certain unity, since they all deal with the conflict, serious and important as Adams thought, between the conclusions of science and the assumptions of historians in respect to the future of man and the world. To these three papers, the editor, Brooks Adams, has contributed an introduction of 125 pages, under the caption of "The Heritage of Henry Adams"; and to the

29

entire volume he has given the title *The Degradation of the Democratic Dogma.**

The title seems ill suited to the papers that make the substance of the volume; but one gathers from the introduction why it was adopted. In the introduction the editor does not concern himself with a criticism of his brother's essays, which he has "long thought unanswerable"; he attempts rather to "tell the story of a movement in thought which has, for the last half century, been developing" in his family. This movement in thought starts with John Quincy Adams, whose life-work was founded on the belief in God and in democracy. To-day, whatever may have happened to the belief in God, the tendency is still "very strong throughout the world to deify the democratic dogma, and to look to democracy to accomplish pretty promptly some approach to a millennium among men." But in the Adams family the belief that democracy, with whatever aid from science, can bring in any millennium has gradually vanished. How it weakened and disappeared is what Brooks Adams tells us in the introduction. Even John Quincy Adams, whose confidence in the value of science was conditioned on his belief in God, died "declaring that God had abandoned him." With God gone, Henry and Brooks, inheriting their grandfather's faith in science, at last came to realize that science taught that neither the world, nor "man as a part of the world, has been evolved in obedience to any single power which might be called a unified creator." On the contrary, science teaches complexity rather than

---

* Review first published in *The American Historical Review*, XXV (April 1920), 480–482; reprinted by permission of *The American Historical Review*.

unity, and a degradation rather than a raising of vital energy. Hence, democracy must partake of the "complexity of its infinitely complex creator, and ultimately end in chaos." The degradation of the democratic dogma which is here in question is thus far from being a general movement of thought; it is a movement within the Adams family, exemplified chiefly in Brooks and Henry.

The three essays of Henry Adams, of which the introduction gives us the genesis, form a valuable supplement to the *Education of Henry Adams,* in so far as that book deals with his effort to formulate for himself an intelligible philosophy of history. The problem which confronted him is stated at length in the *Letter to American Teachers of History.* Science teaches that the universe, in its material and vital processes, is but the expression of an energy, force, will—call it what you like—which, in doing work, is always dissipated, and which must therefore, finally—in some millions of years—be altogether exhausted, the conclusion of which is that humanity is assured of an ever onward and downward movement toward the final equilibrium of death and extinction. Historians, on the other hand, like politicians, teach, or at least assume, an endless "progress" or "evolution" toward a more perfect, or at all events a better "fitted," society. According to Adams, this notion is an illusion; and he wished to impress upon historians the necessity of squaring their account with the conclusions of science. "If the entire universe, in every variety of active energy, organic and inorganic, human or divine, is to be treated as clockwork that is running down, society can hardly go on ignoring the fact forever." He felt strongly, therefore, that historians should deal with their subject on the basis

of assumptions, and by methods, that scientists could recognize as valid. The new essay on "The Rule of Phase Applied to History" is a tentative effort to suggest such assumptions and such methods, an attempt to treat the vital energies that find expression in European history in terms of the Rule of Phase as the physicists understand it.

No extended criticism of Henry Adams' proposed solution of this old riddle can be undertaken in a brief review; but it may be well to suggest that such a criticism would raise at least two questions. The first is this: How does it happen that a mind so critical of all religious and political dogmas could have accepted so readily, so naïvely, the dogmas of natural science? In the eighteenth century men confidently expected that science would reveal for them the secrets of the universe and read the riddle of human life. This was evidently still the hope of John Quincy Adams. At a later day men like Huxley once more proclaimed the scientific evangel. But in recent years professional scientists have generally been more and more disposed to leave sweeping generalizations to laymen. "Science," says Lloyd Morgan,[1] "deals exclusively with changes of configuration, and traces the accelerations which are observed to occur, leaving to metaphysics to deal with the underlying agency, if it exists." The truth is that Henry Adams was by no means content with "science" as Lloyd Morgan defines it. True to his Puritan traditions, he was bound to seek and to find this "underlying agency"; and having lost the God of his fathers, he constructed a new one out of "lines of force." His quarrel with historians is that they will not bow down and wor-

[1] *The Interpretation of Nature,* p. 58.

ship this new God, not of science, but of Henry Adams. And this leads to the second question: Are not historians, in their dealing with human activities, more "scientific" than they would be if they adopted the attitude of Henry Adams? It is a pure assumption on his part that historians teach, or assume, a philosophy of progress. So far as my experience goes, most of them neither teach nor assume such a philosophy. No doubt there are exceptions. Last spring, sitting in a committee appointed to formulate a new history curriculum for schools, I listened to a young man describing with great enthusiasm a proposed new course designed to show the onward and upward progress of democracy—up to and including May 30, 1919. While he was expounding, my eye fell upon the cover of the *Current History* for that very month, and there I read the following words: "Seething Caldron in Europe—Revolution—Civil War—Disorders—Anarchy!" I wondered if I was expected to teach the progress of democracy onward and upward to the Seething Caldron. I decided I wouldn't. On the other hand, when I am invited to "treat the history of modern Europe and America as a typical example of energies undergoing degradation with a headlong rapidity towards inevitable death," I equally decline to teach that. I am content to follow the more modest plan of Lloyd Morgan, to regard the history of modern Europe as a series of "changes in configuration," and to attempt to understand, not in terms of physics, but in terms of human needs, purposes, and acts, how these changes of configuration came about, leaving it to metaphysicians like Henry Adams to deal with the underlying agency, if it exists, and to determine, if they can, whether we are headed for the ash-

heap or the millennium. The ash-heap, even on Henry Adams' calculation, is some millions of years distant; and there is good reason to think that the millennium, if that is to be our fate, is still sufficiently remote not to call for immediate preparation on our part. Whatever its ultimate end or its absolute value may be, and whether we know the ultimate end and the absolute value or whether we know them not, human life will remain essentially what it has been, and will have the same finite and human values and meaning. It is the function of history, as I understand it, to deal with this meaning and these values as they are revealed in the thought and acts of men.

On Writing History

IN 1912 James Harvey Robinson published a little book
entitled *The New History.* Defining history as a study
of man in the past, he said that historians know much
about the past but little about man. He urged them, for
their souls' sake, to learn something about man by acquiring a speaking acquaintance with the newer sciences of
mankind—anthropology, archaeology, psychology, and
some other sciences the names of which I have forgotten.
Adequately equipped with such knowledge, the historian
would be able, he thought, to tell us something more
worth while about man in the past than "whether Charles
the Fat was at Ingelheim or Lustnau on July 1, 887." He
would be able, in fact, to write a "new history," a history
which would "turn on the past and exploit it in the
interest of advance." *

I waited hopefully for the appearance of one of these
new histories. Not that there was any lack of old ones

* A review of Harry Elmer Barnes, *The New History and the
Social Studies;* originally published in *The Saturday Review of
Literature,* II (Aug. 15, 1925), 38; reprinted by permission of *The
Saturday Review.*

which exploited the past in the interest of the advance
of something—or someone. I could point out, for example, Voltaire's *Essai,* Grote's *Greece,* Mommsen's
Rome—and many others. But I imagined these were
not examples of the new history which Robinson had
in mind. So I waited for an example of the real new
history. None appeared—at least none that I recognized
as such. It is true, Robinson himself, after some years,
published *The Mind in the Making,* a fascinating book
which I read and reread with great pleasure. But, perhaps
for that reason, I never took it to be a history, new or
old. Filled with ideas, written with charm and humor,
it was such a book as might be written by a historian
of intelligence who had studied much, experienced much,
reflected much, and who, forgetting for the moment that
he was a historian, said what he thought as well as he
could. Not that I am a stickler for names. Call the book
history if you like. That would even be an advantage to
me personally; for in that case I read history—a thing I
have long had a notion I ought to do, being reputed
a historian. But the point is I did not take *The Mind
in the Making* to be history; and I was just settling
comfortably into the belief that there were as yet no
new histories, when Professor Barnes came along and
unsettled me.

For some time past Professor Barnes has been writing
articles about the new history; and now he has gathered
his researches on the subject into a substantial volume. It
is scholarly, a readable, and a useful book. The author
begins by describing the orthodox type of history writing,
the "political and episodical" type, which long was, and
still is, in the ascendant, especially in the universities,

those entrenched citadels of conservatism. But, it appears, "there are numerous signs that the current political and episodical type of history is gravely threatened"; for there is not only a "newer history," but many newer historians who hold "that the purpose of history is to give the present generation such a complete and reliable picture of the past that it will be able to arrive at an intelligent comprehension of how and why the present state of civilization came about." Historians have no doubt long professed this to be their object (the doctrine was preached to me thirty years ago in college); but they have hitherto failed in attaining this object, one of the chief reasons, according to Professor Barnes, being their lamentable ignorance of the contributions of many social sciences to human knowledge. The new "synthetic" history requires that the historian should take all knowledge, or nearly all, for his province; and the chief purpose of Professor Barnes is to introduce the historian to those sciences with which he ought to be familiar. He therefore proceeds to give, in successive chapters, learnedly and adequately (so I assume, not knowing the literature of these fields) a survey of recent literature in the fields of geography, psychology, anthropology, sociology, science, economics, politics, and ethics. Each chapter closes with a consideration of the relation of the particular science to history, and the book itself closes with a summary chapter on History and Social Intelligence. The volume is essentially an admirable bibliographical survey of the current trend of thought in the social sciences, accompanied by valuable suggestions as to the significance of these sciences for the historian.

Excellent book though it is, I confess it leaves me more

uncertain about the new history than I was. Far from being as yet no new histories, it seems that there are in fact an immense number. Among historians mentioned as having made contributions to the new history, I find: Helmolt, Teggart, Petrie, Breasted, Rogers, Jastrow, Olmstead, Zimmern, Wheeler, Beloch, Duruy, Ferrero, Freeman, Webster, Oman, Jullian, Riehl, Freytag, Treitschke, Lamprecht, Breysig, Rambaud, Wallace, Kluchevsky, Mavor, Green, Shepherd, Abbott, Bolton, Payne, Fox, Schlesinger, Hulbert, Turner, Beard, Dodd, Schmoller, Sombart, Seignobos, Burckhardt, Pollard, Marvin, Vinogradoff, Maitland, Shotwell, Poole, Lecky, Dill, Rashdall, Morley, Benn, Merz, Bury, Acton, Gooch—I started out to make a complete list; but it would take too long. Most interesting of all, I find my own name in repeated and honorable association with the newer historians. Thus it seems that for a hundred years and more there have been any number of newer historians and new histories. While naïvely waiting for the appearance of even one new history, I was myself writing the new history. And so I ask are there any orthodox still living? I should like to meet them in order to gather the oral tradition of a rapidly vanishing method.

All my ideas on the new history being thus unsettled by Professor Barnes's excellent book, I take refuge in the lazy notion that the classification of historians into old and new is neither very informing nor very useful. Besides, it has its practical difficulties. For example. Professor Haskins formerly made careful researches into the institutions, chiefly political of medieval Normandy. He has recently published excellent studies on medieval

science. And I recall a brilliant book of his on *The Normans in Europe*—a work which might well be called "synthetic history." Well, how shall I classify him? Does he belong to the new or the old school? Is he orthodox or heretic? Is he a political, a social, or an intellectual historian? Not knowing how otherwise to classify Professor Haskins, I am content to say merely that he is a thoroughly competent scholar who has chosen to study certain special aspects of the past life of man, and has written admirable books—admirable that is in their kind, not admirable in some other kind.

It is true I am not much interested in the political institutions of medieval Normandy. Are Professor Haskins's studies in that field therefore merely competent exercises in barren antiquarianism? I cannot answer that question. Professor Barnes seems to be rather certain of the grand objective of historical studies. Not being so sure myself, I do not ask any historian, or any group of historians, to prepare a "complete picture of the past" to the end that the present generation may comprehend "how and why the present state of civilization came about." I do not ask the historian to do this, because I think it is impossible to do it. I prefer, with James Harvey Robinson, to "find solace and intellectual repose in surrendering all attempts to define history, and in conceding that it is the business of the historian to find out anything about mankind in the past which he believes to be interesting or important and about which there are sources of information." Therefore I do not ask of the historian that he write new history rather than old, psychological rather than political; I ask only that

he write a good book about something that interests him. This is asking a good deal, but it is not asking the impossible.

What the historian will chiefly need in order to write a good book is intelligence, experience of men and things, insight into human conduct, literary ability, and last but not least knowledge (the more the better, whether of the newer or the older sciences of mankind), knowledge of the subject matter first of all, and then of anything in heaven or earth that may have a bearing on it. Knowing the newer sciences of geography, anthropology, psychology, sociology, politics, economics, and ethics, or some part of them, may indeed be useful. But the systematic mastery of so many disciplines is not for all. It requires the encyclopaedic and the co-ordinating type of mind. Professor Barnes has this type of mind. He has acquired this comprehensive knowledge. He has made good use of it. I hope he will now make a still better use of it by writing a new history, instead of writing more articles and books telling us how to write the new history.

What Are

Historical Facts?

HISTORY is a venerable branch of knowledge, and the writing of history is an art of long standing. Everyone knows what history is, that is, everyone is familiar with the word, and has a confident notion of what it means. In general, history has to do with the thought and action of men and women who lived in past times. Everyone knows what the past is too. We all have a comforting sense that it lies behind us, like a stretch of uneven country we have crossed; and it is often difficult to avoid the notion that one could easily, by turning round, walk back into this country of the past. That, at all events, is what we commonly think of the historian as doing: he works in the past, he explores the past in order to find out what men did and thought in the past. His business is to discover and set forth the "facts" of history.*

* From a manuscript in the Cornell University Archives; first printed in *The Western Political Quarterly*, VIII (Sept. 1955), 327–340; reprinted by permission of the Cornell University Library and *The Western Political Quarterly*. Becker read a version of

When anyone says "facts" we are all there. The word gives us a sense of stability. We know where we are when, as we say, we "get down to the facts"—as, for example, we know where we are when we get down to the facts of the structure of the atom, or the incredible movement of the electron as it jumps from one orbit to another. It is the same with history. Historians feel safe when dealing with the facts. We talk much about the "hard facts" and the "cold facts," about "not being able to get around the facts," and about the necessity of basing our narrative on a "solid foundation of fact." By virtue of talking in this way, the facts of history come in the end to seem something solid, something substantial like physical matter (I mean matter in the common sense, not matter defined as "a series of events in the ether"), something possessing definite shape, and clear persistent outline— like bricks or scantlings; so that we can easily picture the historian as he stumbles about in the past, stubbing his toe on the hard facts if he doesn't watch out. That is his affair of course, a danger he runs; for his business is to dig out the facts and pile them up for someone to use. Perhaps he may use them himself; but at all events he must arrange them conveniently so that someone—perhaps the sociologist or the economist—may easily carry them away for use in some structural enterprise.

Such (with no doubt a little, but not much, exaggeration to give point to the matter) are the common connotations of the words historical facts, as used by historians

___

this essay at the Research Club of Cornell on April 14, 1926, and read it in a slightly revised form at the annual meeting of the American Historical Association at Rochester, New York, December 1926.

and other people. Now, when I meet a word with which I am entirely unfamiliar, I find it a good plan to look it up in the dictionary and find out what someone thinks it means. But when I have frequently to use words with which everyone is perfectly familiar—words like "cause" and "liberty" and "progress" and "government"—when I have to use words of this sort which everyone knows perfectly well, the wise thing to do is to take a week off and think about them. The result is often astonishing; for as often as not I find that I have been talking about words instead of real things. Well, "historical fact" is such a word; and I suspect it would be worthwhile for us historians at least to think about this word more than we have done. For the moment therefore, leaving the historian moving about in the past piling up the cold facts, I wish to inquire whether the historical fact is really as hard and stable as it is often supposed to be.

And this inquiry I will throw into the form of three simple questions. I will ask the questions, I can't promise to answer them. The questions are: (1) What is the historical fact? (2) Where is the historical fact? (3) When is the historical fact? Mind I say *is* not *was*. I take it for granted that if we are interested in, let us say, the fact of the Magna Carta, we are interested in it for our own sake and not for its sake; and since we are living now and not in 1215 we must be interested in the Magna Carta, if at all, for what it is and not for what it was.

First then, What is the historical fact? Let us take a simple fact, as simple as the historian often deals with, viz.: "In the year 49 B.C. Caesar crossed the Rubicon." A familiar fact this is, known to all, and obviously of some importance since it is mentioned in every history

of the great Caesar. But is this fact as simple as it sounds? Has it the clear, persistent outline which we commonly attribute to simple historical facts? When we say that Caesar crossed the Rubicon we do not of course mean that Caesar crossed it alone, but with his army. The Rubicon is a small river, and I don't know how long it took Caesar's army to cross it; but the crossing must surely have been accompanied by many acts and many words and many thoughts of many men. That is to say, a thousand and one lesser "facts" went to make up the one simple fact that Caesar crossed the Rubicon; and if we had someone, say James Joyce, to know and relate all these facts, it would no doubt require a book of 794 pages to present this one fact that Caesar crossed the Rubicon. Thus the simple fact turns out to be not a simple fact at all. It is the statement that is simple—a simple generalization of a thousand and one facts.

Well, anyhow Caesar crossed the Rubicon. But what of it? Many other people at other times crossed the Rubicon. Why charge it up to Caesar? Why for two thousand years has the world treasured this simple fact that in the year 49 B.C. Caesar crossed the Rubicon? What of it indeed? If I, as historian, have nothing to give you but this fact taken by itself with its clear outline, with no fringes or strings tied to it, I should have to say, if I were an honest man, why nothing of it, nothing at all. It may be a fact but it is nothing to us. The truth is, of course, that this simple fact *has* strings tied to it, and that is why it has been treasured for two thousand years. It is tied by these strings to innumerable other facts, so that it can't mean anything except by losing its clear outline. It can't mean anything except as it is absorbed into the complex web

of circumstances which brought it into being. This complex web of circumstances was the series of events growing out of the relation of Caesar to Pompey, and the Roman Senate, and the Roman Republic, and all the people who had something to do with these. Caesar had been ordered by the Roman Senate to resign his command of the army in Gaul. He decided to disobey the Roman Senate. Instead of resigning his command, he marched on Rome, gained the mastery of the Republic, and at last, as we are told, bestrode the narrow world like a colossus. Well, the Rubicon happened to be the boundary between Gaul and Italy, so that by the act of crossing the Rubicon with his army Caesar's treason became an accomplished fact and the subsequent great events followed in due course. Apart from these great events and complicated relations, the crossing of the Rubicon means nothing, is not an historical fact properly speaking at all. In itself it is nothing for us; it becomes something for us, not in itself, but as a symbol of something else, a symbol standing for a long series of events which have to do with the most intangible and immaterial realities, viz.: the relation between Caesar and the millions of people of the Roman world.

Thus the simple historical fact turns out to be not a hard, cold something with clear outline, and measurable pressure, like a brick. It is so far as we can know it, only a *symbol,* a simple statement which is a generalization of a thousand and one simpler facts which we do not for the moment care to use, and this generalization itself we cannot use apart from the wider facts and generalizations which it symbolizes. And generally speaking, the more simple an historical fact is, the more clear and

definite and provable it is, the less use it is to us in and for itself.

Less simple facts illustrate all this equally well, even better perhaps. For example, the fact that "Indulgences were sold in Germany in 1517." This fact can be proved down to the ground. No one doubts it. But taken by itself the fact is nothing, means nothing. It also is a generalization of a thousand and one facts, a thousand and one actions of innumerable sellers and buyers of indulgences all over Germany at many different times; and this also acquires significance and meaning only as it is related to other facts and wider generalizations.

But there are even more indefinite and impalpable facts than these. In the middle of the nineteenth century German historians (and others), studying the customs of the primitive German tribes, discovered a communal institution which they called the German or Teutonic Mark. The German Mark was the product of the historian's fertile imagination working on a few sentences in Caesar's *Gallic Wars* and a few passages in a book called *Germania* written by Tacitus, a disgruntled Roman who tried to get rid of a complex by idealizing the primitive Germans. The German Mark of the historians was largely a myth, corresponding to no reality. The German Mark is nevertheless an historical fact. The idea of the German Mark in the minds of the German historians is a fact in the intellectual history of the nineteenth century—and an important one too. All the elaborate notes I took in college on the German Mark I have therefore long since transferred to those filing cases which contain my notes on the nineteenth century; and there they now repose, side by side with notes on

the Russian Mir, on Hegel's Philosophy of History, on the Positivism of August Comte, on Bentham's greatest good to the greatest number, on the economic theory of the British classical economists, and other illusions of that time.

What then is the historical fact? Far be it from me to define so illusive and intangible a thing! But provisionally I will say this: the historian may be interested in anything that has to do with the life of man in the past —any act or event, any emotion which men have expressed, any idea, true or false, which they have entertained. Very well, the historian is interested in some event of this sort. Yet he cannot deal directly with this event itself, since the event itself has disappeared. What he can deal with directly is a *statement about the event*. He deals in short not with the event, but with a statement which affirms *the fact that the event occurred*. When we really get down to the hard facts, what the historian is always dealing with is an *affirmation*—an affirmation of the fact that something is true. There is thus a distinction of capital importance to be made: the distinction between the ephemeral event which disappears, and the affirmation about the event which persists. For all practical purposes it is this affirmation about the event that constitutes for us the historical fact. If so the historical fact is not the past event, but a symbol which enables us to recreate it imaginatively. Of a symbol it is hardly worthwhile to say that it is cold or hard. It is dangerous to say even that it is true or false. The safest thing to say about a symbol is that it is more or less appropriate.

This brings me to the second question— Where is the historical fact? I will say at once, however brash it sounds,

that the historical fact is in someone's mind or it is no-. where. To illustrate this statement I will take an event familiar to all. "Abraham Lincoln was assassinated in Ford's Theater in Washington on the 14th of April, 1865." That *was* an actual event, occurrence, fact at the moment of happening. But speaking now, in the year 1926, we say it *is* an historical fact. We don't say that it *was* an historical fact, for that would imply that it no longer is one. We say that it *was* an actual event, but *is now* an historical fact. The actual occurrence and the historical fact, however closely connected, are two different things. Very well, if the assassination of Lincoln is an historical fact, where is this fact now? Lincoln is not being assassinated now in Ford's Theater, or anywhere else (except perhaps in propagandist literature!). The actual occurrence, the event, has passed, is gone forever, never to be repeated, never to be again experienced or witnessed by any living person. Yet this is precisely the sort of thing the historian is concerned with—events, acts, thoughts, emotions that have forever vanished as actual occurrences. How can the historian deal with vanished realities? He can deal with them because these vanished realities give place to pale reflections, impalpable images or ideas of themselves, and these pale reflections, and impalpable images which cannot be touched or handled are all that is left of the actual occurrence. These are therefore what the historian deals with. These are his "material." He has to be satisfied with these, for the very good reason that he has nothing else. Well then, where are they—these pale reflections and impalpable images of the actual? Where are these facts? They are, as I said before, in his mind, or in somebody's mind, or they are nowhere.

Ah, but they are in the records, in the sources, I hear someone say. Yes, in a sense, they are in the sources. The historical fact of Lincoln's assassination is in the records —in contemporary newspapers, letters, diaries, etc. In a sense the fact is there, but in what sense? The records are after all only paper, over the surface of which ink has been distributed in certain patterns. And even these patterns were not made by the actual occurrence, the assassination of Lincoln. The patterns are themselves only "histories" of the event, made by someone who had in *his* mind an image or idea of Lincoln's assassination. Of course we, you and I, can, by looking at these inky patterns, form in *our* minds images or ideas more or less like those in the mind of the person who made the patterns. But if there were now no one in the world who could make any meaning out of the patterned records or sources, the fact of Lincoln's assassination would cease to be an historical fact. You might perhaps call it a dead fact; but a fact which is not only dead, but not known ever to have been alive, or even known to be now dead, is surely not much of a fact. At all events, the historical facts lying dead in the records can do nothing good or evil in the world. They become historical facts, capable of doing work, of making a difference, only when someone, you or I, brings them alive in our minds by means of pictures, images, or ideas of the actual occurrence. For this reason I say that the historical fact is in someone's mind, or it is nowhere, because when it is in no one's mind it lies in the records inert, incapable of making a difference in the world.

But perhaps you will say that the assassination of Lincoln has made a difference in the world, and that this difference is now effectively working, even if, for a

moment, or an hour or a week, no one in the world has the image of the actual occurrence in mind. Quite obviously so, but why? Quite obviously because after the actual event people remembered it, and because ever since they have continued to remember it, by repeatedly forming images of it in their mind. If the people of the United States had been incapable of enduring memory, for example, like dogs (as I assume; not being a dog I can't be sure) would the assassination of Lincoln be now doing work in the world, making a difference? If everyone had forgotten the occurrence after forty-eight hours, what difference would the occurrence have made, then or since? It is precisely because people have long memories, and have constantly formed images in their minds of the assassination of Lincoln, that the universe contains the historical fact which persists as well as the actual event which does not persist. It is the persisting historical fact, rather than the ephemeral actual event, which makes a difference to us now; and the historical fact makes a difference only because it is, and so far as it is, in human minds.

Now for the third question— When is the historical fact? If you agree with what has been said (which is extremely doubtful) the answer seems simple enough. If the historical fact is present, imaginatively, in someone's mind, then it is now, a part of the present. But the word present is a slippery word, and the thing itself is worse than the word. The present is an indefinable point in time, gone before you can think it; the image or idea which I have now present in mind slips instantly into the past. But images or ideas of past events are often, perhaps always, inseparable from images or ideas of the

future. Take an illustration. I awake this morning, and among the things my memory drags in to enlighten or distress me is a vague notion that there was something I needed particularly to remember but cannot—a common experience surely. What is it that I needed to remember I cannot recall; but I can recall that I made a note of it in order to jog my memory. So I consult my little pocket memorandum book—a little Private Record Office which I carry about, filled wtih historical sources. I take out my memorandum book in order to do a little historical research; and there I find (Vol. I, p. 20) the dead historical fact— "Pay Smith's coal bill today: $1,016." The image of the memorandum book now drops out of mind, and is replaced by another image —an image of what? Why an image, an idea, a picture (call it what you will) made up of three things more or less inseparable. First the image of myself ordering coal from Smith last summer; second, the image of myself holding the idea in mind that I must pay the bill; third, the image of myself going down to Smith's office at four o'clock to pay it. The image is partly of things done in the past, and partly of things to be done in the future; but it is more or less all one image now present in mind.

Someone may ask, "Are you talking of history or of the ordinary ills of every day that men are heir to?" Well, perhaps Smith's coal bill is only my personal affair, of no concern to anyone else, except Smith to be sure. Take then another example. I am thinking of the Congress of Berlin, and that is without doubt history—the real thing. The historical facts of the Congress of Berlin I bring alive in memory, imaginatively. But I am making an image of the Congress of Berlin for a purpose; and

indeed without a purpose no one would take the trouble to bring historical facts to mind. My purpose happens to be to convey this image of the Congress of Berlin to my class in History 42, in Room C, tomorrow afternoon at 3 o'clock. Now I find that inseparable from this image of the Congress of Berlin, which occurred in the past, are flitting images of myself conveying this image of the Congress of Berlin to my class tomorrow in Room C. I picture myself standing there monotonously talking, I hear the labored sentences painfully issuing forth, I picture the students' faces alert or bored as the case may be; so that images of this future event enter into the imagined picture of the Congress of Berlin, a past event; enter into it, coloring and shaping it too, to the end that the performance may do credit to me, or be intelligible to immature minds, or be compressed within the limits of fifty minutes, or to accomplish some other desired end. Well, this living historical fact, this mixed image of the coal bill or the Congress of Berlin—is it past, present, or future? I cannot say. Perhaps it moves with the velocity of light, and is timeless. At all events it is real history to me, which I hope to make convincing and real to Smith, or to the class in Room C.

I have now asked my three questions, and have made some remarks about them all. I don't know whether these remarks will strike you as quite beside the mark, or as merely obvious, or as novel. If there is any novelty in them, it arises, I think, from our inveterate habit of thinking of the world of history as part of the external world, and of historical facts as actual events. In truth the actual past is gone; and the world of history is an intangible world, re-created imaginatively, and present in our minds.

If, as I think, this is true, then there are certain important implications growing out of it; and if you are not already exhausted I should like to touch upon a few of these implications. I will present them "firstly," "secondly," and so on, like the points of a sermon, without any attempt at co-ordination.

One implication is that by no possibility can the historian present in its entirety any actual event, even the simplest. You may think this a commonplace, and I do too; but still it needs to be often repeated because one of the fondest illusions of nineteenth century historians was that the historian, the "scientific" historian, would do just that: he would "present all the facts and let them speak for themselves." The historian would contribute nothing himself, except the sensitive plate of his mind, upon which the objective facts would register their own unimpeachable meaning. Nietzsche has described the nineteenth-century "objective man" with the acid precision of his inimitable phrases.

The objective man is in truth a mirror: accustomed to prostration before everything that wants to be known, with such desires only as knowing or "reflecting" imply—he waits until something comes, and then expands himself sensitively, so that even the light footsteps and gliding past of spiritual beings may not be lost on his surface and film. Whatever "personality" he still possesses seems to him . . . disturbing; so much has he come to regard himself as the passage and reflection of outside forms and events. . . . Should one wish love or hatred from him . . . he will do what he can, and furnish what he can. But one must not be surprised if it should not be much. . . . His mirroring and eternally self-polishing soul no longer knows how to affirm, no longer how

to deny. . . . He is an instrument . . . but nothing in himself—*presque rien!*

The classical expression of this notion of the historian
as instrument, is the famous statement attributed to
Fustel de Coulanges. Half a century ago the French mind
was reacting strongly against the romantic idea that
political liberty was brought into Gaul by the primitive
Germans; and Fustel was a leader in this reaction. One
day he was lecturing to his students on early French institutions, and suddenly they broke into applause. "Gentlemen," said Fustel, "do not applaud. It is not I who
speak, but history that speaks through me." And all the
time this calm disinterested historian was endeavoring,
with concentrated purpose, to prove that the damned
Germans had nothing to do with French civilization.
That of course was why the students applauded—and
why Fustel told them that it was history that was speaking.

Well, for twenty years I have taken it for granted
that no one could longer believe so preposterous an idea.
But the notion continues to bob up regularly; and only
the other day, riding on the train to the meeting of the
Historical Association, Mr. A. J. Beveridge, eminent and
honored historian, assured me dogmatically (it would be
dogmatically) that the historian has nothing to do but
"present all the facts and let them speak for themselves."
And so I repeat, what I have been teaching for twenty
years, that this notion is preposterous; first, because it is
impossible to present all the facts; and second, because
even if you could present all the facts the miserable things
wouldn't say anything, would say just nothing at all.

Let us return to the simple fact: "Lincoln was assassinated in Ford's Theater, in Washington, April 14, 1865." This is not all the facts. It is, if you like, a *representation* of all the facts, and a representation that perhaps satisfies one historian. But another historian, for some reason, is not satisfied. He says: "On April 14, 1865, in Washington, Lincoln, sitting in a private box in Ford's Theater watching a play, was shot by John Wilkes Booth, who then jumped to the stage crying out, *'Sic semper tyrannis!'*" That is a true affirmation about the event also. It represents, if you like, all the facts too. But its form and content (one and the same thing in literary discourse) is different, because it contains more of the facts than the other. Well, the point is that any number of affirmations (an infinite number if the sources were sufficient) could be made about the actual event, all true, all representing the event, but some containing more and some less of the factual aspects of the total event. But by no possibility can the historian make affirmations describing all of the facts—all of the acts, thoughts, emotions of all of the persons who contributed to the actual event in its entirety. One historian will therefore necessarily *choose* certain affirmations about the event, and relate them in a certain way, rejecting other affirmations and other ways of relating them. Another historian will necessarily make a different choice. Why? What is it that leads one historian to make, out of all the possible true affirmations about the given event, certain affirmations and not others? Why, the purpose he has in his mind will determine that. And so the purpose he has in mind will determine the precise meaning which he derives from the event. The event itself, the facts, do not say anything, do not impose

any meaning. It is the historian who speaks, who imposes a meaning.

A second implication follows from this. It is that the historian cannot eliminate the personal equation. Of course, no one can; not even, I think, the natural scientist. The universe speaks to us only in response to our purposes; and even the most objective constructions, those, let us say, of the theoretical physicist, are not the sole possible constructions, but only such as are found most convenient for some human need or purpose. Nevertheless, the physicist can eliminate the personal equation to a greater extent, or at least in a different way, than the historian, because he deals, as the historian does not, with an external world directly. The physicist presides at the living event, the historian presides only at the inquest of its remains. If I were alone in the universe and gashed my finger on a sharp rock, I could never be certain that there was anything there but my consciousness of the rock and gashed finger. But if ten other men in precisely the same way gash their fingers on the same sharp rock, we can, by comparing impressions, infer that there is something there besides consciousness. There is an external world there. The physicist can gash his finger on the rock as many times as he likes, and get others to do it, until they are all certain of the facts. He can, as Eddington says, make pointer-readings of the behavior of the physical world as many times as he likes for a given phenomenon, until he and his colleagues are satisfied. When their minds all rest satisfied they have an explanation, what is called the truth. But suppose the physicist had to reach his conclusions from miscellaneous records, made by all sorts of people, of experiments that had been

made in the past, each experiment made only once, and none of them capable of being repeated. The external world he would then have to deal with would be the records. That is the case of the historian. The only external world he has to deal with is the records. He can indeed look at the records as often as he likes, and he can get dozens of others to look at them: and some things, some "facts," can in this way be established and agreed upon, as, for example, the fact that the document known as the Declaration of Independence was voted on July 4, 1776. But the meaning and significance of this fact cannot be thus agreed upon, because the series of events in which it has a place cannot be enacted again and again, under varying conditions, in order to see what effect the variations would have. The historian has to judge the significance of the series of events from the one single performance, never to be repeated, and never, since the records are incomplete and imperfect, capable of being fully known or fully affirmed. Thus into the imagined facts and their meaning there enters the personal equation. The history of any event is never precisely the same thing to two different persons; and it is well known that every generation writes the same history in a new way, and puts upon it a new construction.

The reason why this is so—why the same series of vanished events is differently imagined in each succeeding generation—is that our imagined picture of the actual event is always determined by two things: (1) by the actual event itself insofar as we can know something about it; and (2) by our own present purposes, desires, prepossessions, and prejudices, all of which enter into the process of knowing it. The actual event contributes some-

thing to the imagined picture; but the mind that holds the imagined picture always contributes something too. This is why there is no more fascinating or illuminating phase of history than historiography—the history of history: the history, that is, of what successive generations have imagined the past to be like. It is impossible to understand the history of certain great events without knowing what the actors in those events themselves thought about history. For example, it helps immensely to understand why the leaders of the American and French Revolutions acted and thought as they did if we know what their idea of classical history was. They desired, to put it simply, to be virtuous republicans, and to act the part. Well, they were able to act the part of virtuous republicans much more effectively because they carried around in their heads an idea, or ideal if you prefer, of Greek republicanism and Roman virtue. But of course their own desire to be virtuous republicans had a great influence in making them think the Greek and Romans, whom they had been taught to admire by reading the classics in school, were virtuous republicans too. Their image of the present and future and their image of the classical past were inseparable, bound together—were really one and the same thing.

In this way the present influences our idea of the past, and our idea of the past influences the present. We are accustomed to say that "the present is the product of all the past"; and this is what is ordinarily meant by the historian's doctrine of "historical continuity." But it is only a half truth. It is equally true, and no mere paradox, to say that the past (our imagined picture of it) is the product of all the present. We build our conceptions of

history partly out of our present needs and purposes. The past is a kind of screen upon which we project our vision of the future; and it is indeed a moving picture, borrowing much of its form and color from our fears and aspirations. The doctrine of historical continuity is badly in need of overhauling in the light of these suggestions; for that doctrine was itself one of those pictures which the early nineteenth century threw upon the screen of the past in order to quiet its deep-seated fears—fears occasioned by the French Revolution and the Napoleonic wars.

A third implication is that no one can profit by historical research, or not much, unless he does some for himself. Historical knowledge, however richly stored in books or in the minds of professors of history, is no good to me unless I have some of it. In this respect, historical research differs profoundly from research in the natural sciences, at least in some of them. For example, I know no physics, but I profit from physical researches every night by the simple act of pressing an electric light button. And everyone can profit in this way from researches in physics without knowing any physics, without knowing even that there is such a thing as physics. But with history it is different. Henry Ford, for example, can't profit from all the historical researches of two thousand years, because he knows so little history himself. By no pressing of any button can he flood the spare rooms of his mind with the light of human experience.

A fourth implication is more important than the others. It is that every normal person does know some history, a good deal in fact. Of course we often hear someone say: "I don't know any history; I wish I knew

some history; I must improve my mind by learning some history." We know what is meant. This person means that he has never read any history books, or studied history in college; and so he thinks he knows no history. But it is precisely this conventional notion of history as something external to us, as a body of dull knowledge locked up in books, that obscures its real meaning. For, I repeat (it will bear repeating) every normal person— every man, woman, and child—does know some history, enough for his immediate purposes; otherwise he would be a lost soul indeed. I suppose myself, for example, to have awakened this morning with loss of memory. I am all right otherwise; but I can't remember anything that happened in the past. What is the result? The result is that I don't know who I am, where I am, where to go, or what to do. I can't attend to my duties at the university, I can't read this paper before the Research Club. In short, my present would be unintelligible and my future meaningless. Why? Why, because I had suddenly ceased to know any history. What happens when I wake up in the morning is that my memory reaches out into the past and gathers together those images of past events, of objects seen, of words spoken and of thoughts thought in the past, which are necessary to give me an ordered world to live in, necessary to orient me in my personal world. Well, this collection of images and ideas of things past is history, my command of living history, a series of images of the past which shifts and reforms at every moment of the day in response to the exigencies of my daily living. Every man has a knowledge of history in this sense, which is the only vital sense in which he can have a knowledge of history. Every man has some knowledge

of past events, more or less accurate; knowledge enough, and accurate enough, for his purposes, or what he regards as such. How much and how accurate, will depend on the man and his purposes. Now, the point is that history in the formal sense, history as we commonly think of it, is only an extension of memory. Knowledge or history, insofar as it is living history and not dead knowledge locked up in notebooks, is only an enrichment of our minds with the multiplied images of events, places, peoples, ideas, emotions outside our personal experience, an enrichment of our experience by bringing into our minds memories of the experience of the community, the nation, the race. Its chief value, for the individual, is doubtless that it enables a man to orient himself in a larger world than the merely personal, has the effect for him of placing the petty and intolerable present in a longer perspective, thus enabling him to judge the acts and thoughts of men, his own included, on the basis of an experience less immediate and restricted.

A fifth implication is that the kind of history that has most influence upon the life of the community and the course of events is the history that common men carry around in their heads. It won't do to say that history has no influence upon the course of events because people refuse to read history books. Whether the general run of people read history books or not, they inevitably picture the past in some fashion or other, and this picture, however little it corresponds to the real past, helps to determine their ideas about politics and society. This is especially true in times of excitement, in critical times, in time of war above all. It is precisely in such times that they form (with the efficient help of official propaganda!)

an idealized picture of the past, born of their emotions and desires working on fragmentary scraps of knowledge gathered, or rather flowing in upon them, from every conceivable source, reliable or not matters nothing. Doubtless the proper function of erudite historical research is to be forever correcting the common image of the past by bringing it to the test of reliable information. But the professional historian will never get his own chastened and corrected image of the past into common minds if no one reads his books. His books may be as solid as you like, but their social influence will be nil if people do not read them and not merely read them, but read them willingly and with understanding.

It is, indeed, not wholly the historian's fault that the mass of men will not read good history willingly and with understanding; but I think we should not be too complacent about it. The recent World War leaves us with little ground indeed for being complacent about anything; but certainly it furnishes us with no reason for supposing that historical research has much influence on the course of events. The nineteenth century is often called the age of science, and it is often called the age of history. Both statements are correct enough. During the hundred years that passed between 1814 and 1914 an unprecedented and incredible amount of research was carried on, research into every field of history—minute, critical, exhaustive (and exhausting!) research. Our libraries are filled with this stored-up knowledge of the past; and never before has there been at the disposal of society so much reliable knowledge of human experience. What influence has all this expert research had upon the social life of our time? Has it done anything to restrain the

foolishness of politicians or to enhance the wisdom of statesmen? Has it done anything to enlighten the mass of the people, or to enable them to act with greater wisdom or in response to a more reasoned purpose? Very little surely, if anything. Certainly a hundred years of expert historical research did nothing to prevent the World War, the most futile exhibition of unreason, take it all in all, ever made by civilized society. Governments and peoples rushed into this war with undiminished stupidity, with unabated fanaticism, with unimpaired capacity for deceiving themselves and others. I do not say that historical research is to blame for the World War. I say that it had little or no influence upon it, one way or another.

It is interesting, although no necessary part of this paper, to contrast this negligible influence of historical research upon social life with the profound influence of scientific research. A hundred years of scientific research has transformed the conditions of life. How it has done this is known to all. By enabling men to control natural forces it has made life more comfortable and convenient, at least for the well-to-do. It has done much to prevent and cure disease, to alleviate pain and suffering. But its benefits are not unmixed. By accelerating the speed and pressure of life it has injected into it a nervous strain, a restlessness, a capacity for irritation and an impatience of restraint never before known. And this power which scientific research lays at the feet of society serves equally well all who can make use of it—the harbingers of death as well as of life. It was scientific research that made the war of 1914, which historical research did nothing to prevent, a world war. Because of scientific research it could be, and was, fought with more cruelty and ruthlessness,

and on a grander scale, than any previous war; because of scientific research it became a systematic massed butchery such as no one had dreamed of, or supposed possible. I do not say that scientific research is to blame for the war; I say that it made it the ghastly thing it was, determined its extent and character. What I am pointing out is that scientific research has had a profound influence in changing the conditions of modern life, whereas historical research has had at best only a negligible influence. Whether the profound influence of the one has been of more or less benefit to humanity than the negligible influence of the other, I am unable to determine. Doubtless both the joys and frustrations of modern life, including those of the scholarly activities, may be all accommodated and reconciled within that wonderful idea of Progress which we all like to acclaim—none more so, surely, than historians and scientists.

What Is Historiography?

FORTY years ago I was fascinated by the *study* of history
—the mechanics of research, of that sort of research at
all events (there are other kinds) which has been defined
as "taking little bits out of a great many books that no
one has ever read, and putting them together in one
book that no one will ever read." Later I became less
interested in the study of history than in history itself
—that is to say, in the suggestive meaning that could
be attributed to certain periods or great events, such as
that "the spirit of Rome is an acid which, applied to the
sentiment of nationality, dissolved it," or that "the
Renaissance was the double discovery of man and the
world." Now that I am old the most intriguing aspect
of history turns out to be neither the study of history
nor history itself, in the above noted senses, but rather
the study of the history of historical study. The name
given to this aspect of history is the unlovely one, as Mr.
Barnes says, of Historiography.*

* A review of Harry Elmer Barnes, *History of Historical Writing;* originally published in *The American Historical Review,*
XLIV (Oct. 1938), 20–28; reprinted by permission of *The American Historical Review.*

What precisely is Historiography? It may be, and until recently has for the most part been, little more than the notation of the historical works since the time of the Greeks, with some indication of the purposes and points of view of the authors, the sources used by them, and the accuracy and readability of the works themselves. The chief object of such enterprises in historiography is to assess, in terms of modern standards, the value of historical works for us. At this level historiography gives us manuals of information about histories and historians, provides us, so to speak, with a neat balance sheet of the "contributions" which each historian has made to the sum total of verified historical knowledge now on hand. Such manuals have a high practical value. To the candidate for the Ph.D. they are indeed indispensable, since they provide him at second hand with the most up-to-date information. From them he learns what were the defects and limitations of his predecessors, even the most illustrious, without the trouble of reading their works—as, for example, that Macaulay, although a brilliant writer, was blinded by Whig prejudice, or that Tacitus' estimate of Tiberius has been superseded by later researches, or that Thucydides' trenchant account of the Peloponnesian War suffers from the author's unfamiliarity with the doctrine of the economic interpretation of history. Knowing the limitations of our most famous predecessors gives us all confidence in the value of our own researches: we may not be brilliant, but we can be sound. We have the great advantage of living in more enlightened times: our monographs may never rank with *The Decline and Fall* as literary classics, but they will be based upon sources of information not available

to Gibbon, and made impeccable by a scientific method not yet discovered in his day.

Mr. Harry Elmer Barnes's *History of Historical Writing* is far more than this—more than an annotated catalogue of historical works. Yet in some sense it is this too, a little too much so, more so perhaps than his purpose called for or than he intended. There are parts of the book which left me with little but an envious admiration for the author's erudition, his easy familiarity with the contents of innumerable books of which I had never heard. My first impression indeed, upon finishing the book, was that I could happily find within its covers the name of every historian since the time of Menetho. Of course no real scholar would get any such impression. Not being a learned person, I am easily astounded by anyone who knows the titles of a thousand and one books. But still, I have looked at bibliographies—for example, the *Bibliographie de l'histoire de Paris pendant la Révolution* by Tourneux, in five large volumes; and recalling this impressive work I realize that even the bare titles of all the works on the French Revolution alone could not be contained in Mr. Barnes's small volume. What a list of all the historical writings since the time of Menetho would run to I know not, nor wish to know—a dreadful thought! And so, not to slander Mr. Barnes, I hasten to say that there must be innumerable writers whom he does not mention, and even, I like to think, many whom he has never heard of. He has after all selected only a few, relatively speaking; and he has selected them, even if at times with insufficient restraint, for a definite purpose.

Mr. Barnes states his purpose as follows:—"to char-

acterize the intellectual background of each major period of human advance in western civilization, show how the historical literature of each period has been related to its parent culture, point out the dominant traits of the historical writing in each era, indicate the advance, if any, in historical science, and then make clear the individual contributions of the major historical writers of the age." At this level historiography should be something more than an estimate of the contributions of historians to present knowledge. It should be in some sense a phase of intellectual history, that phase of it which records what men have at different times known and believed about the past, the use they have made, in the service of their interests and aspirations, of their knowledge and beliefs, and the underlying presuppositions which have made their knowledge seem to them relevant and their beliefs seem to them true. The historiographer who wishes to succeed on this level should acquire much precise knowledge, but above all he should cultivate a capacity for imaginative understanding. If he wishes to fail, he should cultivate a capacity for being irritated by the ignorance and foolishness of his predecessors.

How well has Mr. Barnes succeeded in accomplishing his purpose? On the whole, well enough. Mr. Barnes has, to be sure, a certain capacity for being irritated. It is a defect of his quality. He is that rare phenomenon, a learned crusader. He is passionately interested in the application of scientific knowledge to the task of creating the good society. He is profoundly convinced that history, rightly understood, throws much needed light on the causes of the plight in which we find ourselves at the

present moment; convinced, therefore, that historians, if only they would fully emancipate themselves from antiquarianism and bring their knowledge to bear upon present social problems, could contribute much more than they do to the solution of those problems. I suspect that what really irritates Mr. Barnes is after all not the historians but rather the fact that so few people make any effort to appropriate the knowledge available, so many people prefer the *Saturday Evening Post* to the most up-to-date popular works on the social sciences; and this irritation is in part conveniently relieved from time to time by disparaging and opprobrious remarks about "the orthodox historian"—a species supposed to have flourished unashamed before the time of James Harvey Robinson and not yet wholly extinct.

Since the orthodox historian plays a minor role in the present book, a word needs to be said about him. I am not sure that I have ever met the fellow in the flesh. By definition he appears to be a timid, refined professor, a little apprehensive about holding his job, who is interested in political, military, and diplomatic events, is unaware of the importance of economic, social, and cultural influences, and greatly exaggerates the role of individuals as causal factors in the historic process. What puzzles me a little is that on this showing Mr. Barnes himself, although rarely accounted timid and never known to be restrained by the fear of losing his job, can be otherwise orthodox when the occasion calls for it. In his book, *The Genesis of the World War,* I seem to remember, he dealt exclusively with political and diplomatic events and ended by naming four individuals whose nefarious activities were largely responsible for

bringing on the war. What puzzles me still more is the fact that, although from Mr. Barnes's general discussion of the "new history" I should expect virtually all historians prior to the twentieth century to be orthodox, I find in his pages singularly few historians who adhere strictly to the orthodox line. On the contrary, in the chapters on "Social and Cultural History" and "Kulturgeschichte," I find evidence leading me to suppose that the new history is at least as old as Voltaire, and that a great many of the most distinguished historians of the last two centuries have by no means confined their interests to political history or notably exaggerated the role of individuals as causal factors.

It was Freeman who said that "history is past politics," and in his day interest in political and constitutional history was, it is true, very strong. But Mr. Barnes might have found an explanation, very satisfactory to the new historians, I should have thought, of that fact. It was a time when the major problems of society were political and constitutional, a time when revolutions were primarily concerned with the form of government and the construction of the right kind of constitution for guaranteeing the political privileges and imprescriptible natural rights of individuals; and what, then, were these political historians doing if they were not bringing history "to bear on the present," if they were not "exploiting the past in the interest of advance," which, according to James Harvey Robinson, is what the new historian does and all historians should do? Can it be that even Freeman was, in his own day, a newer historian? But Freeman was still alive when the economic interpretation began to make headway, and today I would find it difficult to name a historian of ability who could, according to Mr. Barnes's definition, be rightly

classed with the strictly orthodox. I am grateful to Mr. Barnes for not classing me with the orthodox, partly because I dislike the term on principle, whatever it means, chiefly because I do not like to be outrageously conspicuous. But still I do not mind being thought a little eccentric, and so I will risk the following observation: when the devotion of my colleagues to social history becomes such that a History of American Life can be written with only a perfunctory mention of politics, it is well to remember that politics has after all had something to do, as much at least as sport, with making American life what it is.

But I am making too much of Mr. Barnes's irritations and disgusts. They obtrude only late in the book and are at most only a minor defect. Taking the book as a whole, Mr. Barnes has done well what he set out to do. He has "characterized the intellectual background of each major period," if with no special insight or freshness, at least well enough to enable the reader to understand "the dominant traits of historical writing" in each period—to understand, for example, why historical writing in the Middle Ages necessarily differed from historical writing in classical times, why the Humanists fashioned their histories on Roman models, why the religious disputes of the Reformation turned theologians to the study of church history, and so following. Particularly good in this connection is his notation of the relation between the discovery of new countries and the growing interest in the history of social institutions and his indication of the conditions in the early nineteenth century which stimulated an interest in the philosophy of history.

Nevertheless, the characterization of the "intellectual

background" and the explanation of the "dominant traits
of historical writing" in terms of that background, although for the most part adequate to the author's purpose,
is brief and it must be said somewhat perfunctory; it does
not make the substance of the book. The greater part of
the book is devoted to what interests Mr. Barnes far more
—that is to say, to the "contributions of the major historical writers" and to "the advance, if any, in historical
science." To estimate the value of histories and historians
from the point of view of modern standards and technique
is after all the principal object of the book, and this is after
all what Mr. Barnes does best. Perhaps too many historical
writers are mentioned, so that at times the book degen-
erates into a catalogue of names. "W. R. Shepherd, H. E.
Bolton, W. S. Robertson, J. F. Rippy, Bernard Moses,
C. W. Hackett . . . H. I. Priestley, E. C. Barker and
others"—there is, particularly in the later chapters, far
too much of this sort of thing. Mr. Barnes knows too
much, and when the names begin to swarm in memory he
allows his judgment to retire behind the cloud. He is
better in those earlier, happier times when historians, not
being so numerous, do not venture to gang up on him. He
then finds space to tell us who they were and what they
wrote with sufficient detail to make them and their writings intelligible to us. Learned scholars, not being so
easily put down by Mr. Barnes's erudition as I was, will
find errors here and there and some mistaken or question-
able judgments. But so far as I know, Mr. Barnes's
knowledge is adequate, and his estimates, if mostly conventional, are on the whole, perhaps for that reason,
essentially sound. No doubt it is beside the point to de-
plore the fact that "Thucydides neglected the magnificent

opportunity to portray the glories of Athenian civilization." No doubt less than justice is done to Flacius
Illyricus and his collaborators by stressing their "gullibil-
ity" and not sufficiently emphasizing the fact that in sub-
stituting tradition for formal logic as a test of religious
doctrine and practice they were giving an immense im-
petus to the development of historical studies. But these
are small points. On the whole Mr. Barnes has made an
important addition to the literature of historiography. He
has written, not an "epoch-making" book, not a profoundly original book (few books can be rightly so described), but a sound and useful book—for those not too
familiar with the history of historical writing, the most
informative and stimulating book, I should think, now
available in English.

An author should be conceded his intention and judged
by the success he attains in realizing it. For this reason I
do not say of Mr. Barnes, as he says of Thucydides, that he
has missed a magnificent opportunity. Nevertheless, the
opportunity, whether magnificent or not, is there for
those who wish to embrace it. It would be worth while, I
should think, to regard historiography more simply, more
resolutely, as a phase of intellectual history; to forget
entirely about the contributions of historians to present
knowledge and to concentrate wholly upon their role in
the cultural pattern of their own time. From this point of
view the historiographer would be primarily concerned
with what Professor Shotwell happily calls mankind's
gradual "discovery of Time" or, more broadly, with the
gradual expansion of the time and space frame of reference which in some fashion conditions the range and
quality of human thought.

When we think of anything, we think of it in relation to other things located in space and occurring in time, that is to say, in a time and space world, a time and space frame of reference. The development of intelligence, in the individual and the race, is in some sense a matter of pushing back the limits of the time and space world and filling it with things that really exist and events that actually happened. The time and space world of the new-born child, for example, is confined to the room in which he lies and to the present moment: everything that he observes is seen as a close-up, unrelated to anything else. The earliest men were like new-born children, knowing nothing of any country beyond the region in which they lived, nothing, or very little and that little mostly wrong, about any past events in which they had not taken part. They too saw things as close-ups, in short perspective, unrelated to any verifiable objects in distant places or past times. The ancient Sumerians were in many ways a highly civilized people, but their social thinking was hampered by the fact that they lived in a very narrow time and space world: in their space world the human race could be destroyed by a flood sweeping the valley of the Two Rivers; in their time world the outstanding event was the Great Flood, before which stretched an unknown period, empty of content save for the eight kings believed to have reigned during 241,000 years. From the time of the Sumerians to our own day the human race has slowly and painfully extended the time and space world in which it could live, the time and space frame of reference in which it could think. The spaciousness and content of the time and space frame of reference, far more than sheer brain power, have determined the range and direction of intelligence and the

underlying presuppositions that so largely shape the ideas of men about their relations to the universe and to each other.

Regarded strictly as a phase of intellectual history and not as a balance sheet of verifiable historical knowledge, historiography would have as its main theme the gradual expansion of this time and space world (particularly the time world perhaps, although the two are inseparably connected), the items, whether true or false, which acquired knowledge and accepted beliefs enabled men (and not historians only) to find within it, and the influence of this pattern of true or imagined events upon the development of human thought and conduct. So regarded, historiography would become a history of history rather than a history of historians, a history of history subjectively understood (the "fable agreed upon," the "pack of tricks played on the dead") rather than a history of the gradual emergence of historical truth objectively considered. The historiographer would of course be interested in histories—they would be a main source of information; but he would not confine his researches to them—would not, indeed, be interested in histories as such but only as one of the literary forms in which current ideas about the past find expression. Nor would he be more interested in true than in false ideas about the past: his aim would be to know what ideas, true or false, were at any time accepted and what pressure they exerted upon those who entertained them. He would not then dismiss the *Epic of Gilgamesh* or Homer's *Iliad* as irrelevant for history because they are a collection of myths or be content to say of Livy that he is a good story teller but a bad historian. Not being primarily concerned with what the Romans actually

knew about the past but with what they had in mind when they thought about it, he would seize upon the *fact* that Livy wrote his history, the *fact* that the myths it relates were current and widely accepted as true. He would realize that while a myth may not be true, that it exists is true, and that people believe it, is true and may be of the highest importance. In short, the "facts" that would concern the historiographer, the "what actually happened" that he would look for and find relevant to his purpose, would be, not the truth, but the existence and pressure of the ideas about the past which men have entertained and acted upon. His object would be to reconstruct, and by imaginative insight and aesthetic understanding make live again, that pattern of events occurring in distant places and times past which, in successive periods, men have been able to form a picture of when contemplating themselves and their activities in relation to the world in which they live. Whether the events composing the pattern are true or false, objectively considered, need not concern him.

Taken in this sense, historiography should no doubt begin with "pre-historic times"—an absurd term, as Mr. Barnes says, if we are to regard history externally, as the record of what men have done, since it implies that by far the longest span of human history occurred before there was any history. But not so absurd after all if we are to think of history from the inside, as a possession of the mind, as the developing apprehension of the past and of distant places, since the earliest men could have had very little history in that sense. Yet even the earliest men (the Cro-Magnons, for example) must have been able to form some picture, however limited in design and blurred in detail, of what had occurred and was occurring in the

world. What this picture was we can only guess, although some ingenious and even illuminating guesses could no doubt be brought to birth by the anthropologists. The historiographer could at all events begin with the oldest epic stories—the Babylonian *Creation Epic,* Homer's *Iliad,* and the like. For the early Greeks the *Iliad,* as someone has said (Matthew Arnold perhaps?), was history, story, and scripture all in one. Such differentiating terms are of course misleading, since we may be fairly sure that the early Greeks made no such distinctions. The story as told—the siege of Troy, the doings of men and gods—was all real, history simply, the record of what actually happened. And so of all people whose civilization developed directly out of primitive conditions.

Not until written records had been long in use could men become effectively conscious of the fact that the event as recorded differs from the event as remembered. Then only could they properly distinguish between story and history—between the account of events imaginatively invented and the account of events that actually happened; then only could histories be thought of as a "branch of literature." But the differentiation of history and literature does not at once make the gods indispensable. Inscrutable in their purposes, implacable in their judgments, rulers of men and things, the gods are still necessary: necessary for literature because they are so intimately involved in the current affairs of men; necessary for history because the creation of the world has to be accounted for, and men, even the ancient heroes and godlike kings, are incapable of so great a task. History therefore long remains entangled with religion, the gods serving as causal agencies operating behind men and events. But as the time and space world is expanded,

providing an ever greater variety of novel items for comparison and appraisal, philosophy intrudes with its abstractions; and the gods, withdrawing from the immediate affairs of men to the place where absolute being dwells, fade away into pale replicas of their former selves —into the Law of Nature, the Transcendent Idea, the dynamic principle of Dialectic, or whatever it may be. Philosophy in turn becomes Natural Philosophy, then Natural Science, then Science: and science, dispensing altogether with the assistance of the gods and their numerous philosophic progeny, presents for contemplation the bare record of how as a matter of fact the outer world behaves, of what as a matter of fact has occurred in past times, leaving man alone in an indifferent universe without attempting to justify its ways to his deeds and aspirations.

This theme, or something like it, has been played, with appropriate variations, more than once—by the Greeks, by the Romans, by the Europeans in modern times. What is the relation between the development of an industrial-commercial society, the decline of traditional religious and political convictions, and the growth of skepticism and scientific knowledge? How can these related phenomena be correlated with the time and space world in which men live, the time and space frame of reference in which they think? What place has history, regarded as the *sense of the past,* as the apprehension of events, true or false, that are thought to have occurred or to be occurring in distant places and times past, in this correlation both as cause and effect? Within the range of these questions are to be found, I venture to think, many fruitful fields for the historiographer to cultivate.

Letters on History

1. CARL BECKER TO WILLIAM E. DODD

*Carl Becker and William E. Dodd became acquainted while Becker was teaching at the University of Kansas and Dodd was teaching at the University of Chicago. Becker wrote a volume—*The Beginnings of the American People *(1915)— for an American history series that Dodd edited, and the two became lifelong friends, who found each other congenial even when in disagreement. The following letter on the need of a subtle psychology rather than a rigorous definition of terms in dealing with the past was written about 1923.*

MY DEAR DODD,

Your letter interested me much, and the inclosed separate, which I think I have already read, I read again with great pleasure, and with agreement. I saw [Charles M.?] Andrews last summer, and he raised the question of my statements in the "Eve of the Revolution" [and] "Dem. an Experiment." * We discussed the matter for some time, and I did not see that we differed much except that he

* *The Eve of the Revolution* (New Haven: Yale University Press, 1919); *The United States: An Experiment in Democracy* (New York: Harper, 1920).

79

thought I had used the term democracy without considering whether that was the precise term that they would
have used, or rather whether they would have meant by
government by the people just what we mean by the word
democracy. He did say that he thought the Revolution
had been entirely misconceived, and was writing, or pre-
paring to write, a book which would give a different view.
I really don't think he has anything new. Of course there
were plenty of people who supported the Revolution and
used the conventional ideology while it was going on, who
did not relish government by the people much, just as
there were plenty of people who thrilled with pride and
emotion when President Wilson's fine words were quoted
in 1917–18, and quite sincerely, who nevertheless were
ready to think in 1920 that it was all idealistic and "visionary." In both states of mind they were quite sincere—I am
speaking now of thousands of the plain people who don't
think very much or consistently about these things. The
truth is few people care much for equality unless they are
trying to climb up to the other fellow's level. Andrews'
discussion of whether people in 1776 really wanted democracy or not struck me as largely futile, because it
missed the point that democracy or aristocracy are, like
war, not objects in themselves which people want or don't
want; people want or don't want a great variety of things,
against which or for which they struggle, and war, democracy, etc., are instruments, sometimes no more than words,
which they lay hold upon as a means of obtaining what
they want or safeguarding them against what they don't
want. Thousands of people now lay hold of the word
democracy as a safeguard against Bolshevism, democracy
being of course the word which describes the government

we have and which they are satisfied with. If the danger of Bolshevism disappeared and they suddenly found themselves pinched by the Beef Trust, they would easily turn round and demand a democratic government in place of government by the interests. Very few people think with their minds. That is an unusual accomplishment, like objectivity, or always telling the exact truth, or reading a foreign language. People commonly think with their emotions; and these periods of ebb and flow which you point out in our history are, I think, less the results of a more or less effective struggle of the people consciously aiming at democracy than they are the result of shifting emotional reactions of the same people, or the same kind of people. I don't see history quite as much in terms of a conscious class struggle of conflicting economic interests, as you seem to do. People's minds are far too muddled to carry on any such struggle for more than a short time. Besides the overwhelming majority of people give on an average only an infinitesimal part of their time to social or political aims or thought. You can take any average man and find that on one side of his mind, if you introduce the subject in the right way, he is a democrat, but introduce the subject in another way and you will find another side of his mind which is pure aristocrat. But he is not conscious of any inconsistency. What historical research needs is a more subtle psychology.

With apologies,

CARL BECKER

2. CARL BECKER TO F. S. RODKEY

F. S. Rodkey, Professor of History at the University of Illinois, was an undergraduate student of Carl Becker's at the University of Kansas from 1914–1916. In 1933 Rodkey sent an article (later privately published as "An Historical Approach to the World Problems of Today") to Becker for criticism, suggesting that perhaps his article was too radical.

[Received November 27, 1933]

DEAR RODKEY,

I don't think your article is very "radical." But what if it were? I wouldn't bother to ask that question. In so far as you are concerned with the question of whether your ideas are too radical or too conservative, you are letting your mind wander from the essential point, which is whether they are true or false, valid or invalid. I think in fact your ideas are very sound. They are apparently: (1) that the changes that may be necessary and that will be practicable depend upon a certain heritage which is vastly different than that of Russia; (2) that the objective of the Communist ideology, whatever may be said of its practice in Russia, is a more equalitarian & democratic society; (3) that this ideology is not essentially different from our own democratic ideology; (4) that therefore it should be possible for us to achieve that objective without resort to the violent revolutionary methods that have been applied in Russia.

This is all very good. I think, however, you have made it rather heavy reading and not as clear as you might by building your exposition around a clumsy academic terminology—*Dialectic Materialism*, "Mechanistic determinism" and the like. Also by some rather involved and slow-moving

sentences. I don't know for whom this paper is intended; but it won't mean very much to the average person. You mention presenting such a point of view to the "man on the street." For him it would have to be put much simpler. And the less said about Russia and dialectic materialism the better. We might very well in 25 years or so come out with a regulated economy not very different from that which may prevail in Russia then. But if we do it we will have to avoid carefully the Communist terminology & invent a new one. In fact we are already doing it. *National Industrial Recovery Act:* What could be more American or less alarming. These are all familiar words, saturated with American feeling. But Soviet, Communism, Marxism, Bolshevism, Dialectic Materialism—these words will not go down.

Professors are apt to be convinced, naturally enough, that great social changes can be brought about by deliberation & rational reflection. This is a great mistake. The average person—& this means 90%—cannot think at all in general terms. He can think pretty sensibly about specific concrete matters that touch him personally. It is the pressure of economic distress that alone has made it possible even to attempt anything that looks in the direction of a nationally planned or supervised economy. And such support as this attempt has had has been elicited, not because people understand intellectually what is being done or attempted, but because their emotions & their hopes have been mobolized. The N R A has been put over, in so far as it has been, in the same way precisely as the war was put over—that is, by appealing to people's "loyalty," by getting them to feel that they must "stand back of" the President, & that to criticize or question (that is to delib-

erate rationally & try to get at the merits of the scheme) is to be a "reactionary," a "Tory," etc. People can understand and enjoy a boycott much better than an argument.

Well, I think the N.R.A. is good if it is a beginning; but if it is to be only a beginning it is no good. We will have to go much farther in regulating our industrial system if we are to avoid worse things. The crux of the matter is *profits*. What is to be done with profits that machines pile up & now place in the control of a few private persons. These have got to be distributed, not directly but indirectly, in such a way as to enable the man of the people to buy what is essential. Even the capitalist himself ought to be intelligent enough to see that there is no use making millions of motor cars, even with the latest radiator caps, unless people have money in their pocket to buy them. How this management of profits is to be effected I don't know, but it can only be done from the point of view of the social interest. It won't do any longer to leave it to a few private gamblers & guessors. I hope we can do it without suppression of the traditional right of discussion & criticism. If we can't we shall have lost the best thing we have; & in the long run I think it will never be done successfully by choking off all ideas except those that square with an established & official dogma.

Sincerely
CARL BECKER

3. CARL BECKER TO LOUIS GOTTSCHALK

Louis Gottschalk, Professor of History at the University of Chicago, was an undergraduate and graduate student of Carl Becker's at Cornell from 1917–1921. In 1938 Gottschalk pub-

lished an article entitled "Leon Trotsky and the Natural History of Revolutions" (American Journal of Sociology, *XLIV* [*Nov. 1938*], *339–354*). *Becker commented on the article in the following letter.*

December 26, 1938

DEAR GOTTSCHALK,

. . . . I have just read your article on Trotsky. Very acute, without being unjust to Trotsky. I confess not to know what a revolution can be, apart from the historical events which exhibit it; & in that sense no revolution is ever betrayed. What is betrayed are the hopes & expectations of leaders who wish it might have taken another course. In this sense every revolution is betrayed, because history is a cynical, tough old nut that always betrays our ideal aspirations. In the case of the Russian revolution history betrayed the Marxist utopian dream, just as in the French Revolution history betrayed the liberal democratic dream of equality & fraternity. Your point about Trotsky's attitude towards Kerensky etc. is very well taken. Marxists ought, on their own theory of the class struggle, to take it for granted that the bourgeois classes will fight for their interests. Christian, or even liberal philosophy, would justify me, for example, in sacrificing my interests for the welfare of mankind; but on the basis of Marxian philosophy, I would be a fool to work for Communism. I am a professor, that is to say a tool of Capitalism which supports me; and why should I not, therefore, fight for my class & my own interests. . . .

Sincerely,
CARL BECKER

4. CARL BECKER TO LOUIS GOTTSCHALK

In 1944 Louis Gottschalk published an article on "Causes of Revolution" (American Journal of Sociology, L [July 1944], 1–8). Becker commented on the article in the following letter.

September 3, 1944

DEAR GOTTSCHALK,

Thanks for your article on Causes of Revolution. I think what you say suits me as well as any description could. I like particularly your emphasis on the fact that we can't count on people *not learning* from experience. That puts it in the safest way no doubt. But by & large the fundamental difference between the social studies and the natural sciences, or perhaps I should say the physical sciences, is that the subject matter of the latter cannot change its habits by learning, while the subject matter of the social studies can & does change its habits by learning. And the important thing is that part of this learning is learning what the social scientist or historian has discovered about its behavior in the past. Hence you may say that any theory about the behavior of man in the past, in so far as men accept it and act on it, falsifies the theory because it introduces a new condition into the factors that determine the behavior of men in the future. The Marxian theory had this effect because millions of men accepted it as true whether it was or not, & for that reason acted differently than they would have done if the theory had never been published. If Marx wanted his theory to remain valid (supposing it was valid for the past) for the future, he should have kept it to himself. I have expressed this differ-

ence by saying that "fortunately for the physicist the atom cannot acquire a knowledge of physics."

Of course the concept of "cause" is a difficult one to define. There is always as you say the question of what is the cause of the cause, & this takes you back to the first cause, which leaves the question unanswered. The physicist therefore dispenses with the concept altogether, & is content to describe sequences and relations, reducing them to mathematics whenever possible. But the historian cannot dispense with cause, except in so far as he is a mere antiquarian or statistician. I think the reason is that he deals not only with the action of men, but with their purposes, desires, aspirations, etc. That is men's actions have value & purpose; and if we write history in such a way as to give it meaning and significance we have to take account of these values & purposes, to explain *why* men behave as they do, what they aim to accomplish, & whether they succeed or not. In explaining all this we use "cause" in the same way we do in practical life—as, for example the cause of missing my train was that my watch was slow. In history therefore, our causes are not on the scientific level or the philosophical level, but on the practical level of every day life. They are our best estimates or judgments. The cause of the French Rev[olution] must therefore in this sense be multiple, and they will differ according to the historian & according to the age in which he writes. This does not mean that historians at any time can't reach a degree of agreement, but one historian will emphasize one factor more than another. It is rare that you can place your finger on one factor and say that without this the Rev[olution] would not have occurred. You can come close to explain-

ing the American Civil War. You can say with confidence, I think, that without the presence of Negro slavery the Civil War would not have occurred. American historians have been too clever by half in finding other causes of the Civil War. Of course you can say that even with slavery if people had not come to regard it as a moral evil there would not have been the "irrepressible conflict" over it, & so no war. But if there had been no slavery there would have been no occasion for thinking about it as an evil. The only way you can eliminate slavery as the fundamental cause, is to ask what were the causes of slavery existing in the U.S. & of course this takes you on the long trek through the dark backward & abysm of time to the ultimate cause of all things—which is of no use to the historian.

Well, I like your article very much. You have evidently given a lot of thought to this subject. . . .

Sincerely

CARL BECKER

II

ON EDUCATION

On Being a Professor

Some Remarks on Education by One Whose
Early Training Was Not of the Best

SOCRATES. About what does the Sophist make a man eloquent? The player on the lyre may be supposed to make a
man eloquent about that which he understands, that is about
playing the lyre. Is not that so?

HIPPOCRATES. Yes.

SOCRATES. Then about what does the Sophist make him
eloquent? Must not he make him eloquent in that which he
understands?

HIPPOCRATES. Yes, that may be assumed.

SOCRATES. And what is that which the Sophist knows and
makes his disciple know?

HIPPOCRATES. Indeed, that I cannot tell.

I

A MINOR use of newspapers and magazines is that they
often convey information about a man which the man
himself would never acquire by observation and experience alone. It was in this way, through the invaluable

91

pages of the *Atlantic Monthly* and other periodicals, that
I first learned of the forlorn state of that ancient, and once
honorable, company of College Professors. Notwithstand-
ing the unselfish devotion with which they pursue a noble
calling, so at least I was led to infer, Professors are frequently without influence in their own communities, only
by close and even humiliating economies have occasionally
a little free pocket money, and generally speaking are unable, for financial reasons mainly, to cultivate the tranquil
mind or properly to nourish what the Germans call the
inner life. Having myself been a professor for some years,
plodding along contentedly enough for the most part, I
was extremely sorry to hear—as I say from the periodicals
—of my present lamentable situation.*

How I came to join this unfortunate class may perhaps
be of some sociological interest, particularly so since my
earliest impression of the professor should have prejudiced
me for life against the calling. It was as a lad that I came to
know a lean little old man, in ancient shiny frock coat,
who came every Spring to prepare our firewood. He sawed
wood for a living; but by profession was a weather prophet.
When he went down the street people were expected to
observe him. If he went freehanded you were to know that
the day would be fine; but he reserved a plentiful supply
of biting sarcasm for those who ventured forth unpro-
tected, even on a cloudless day, after having seen him pass
with an umbrella. He was an excellent wood-sawyer; but
it was the common belief in the community that as a
weather prophet he was visionary, an incurable idealist,
inefficient certainly to the last degree, and of no practical

* An essay first published in the *Unpopular Review*, VII (April
1917), 342–361; reprinted by permission of Henry Holt and Company.

use whatever. In fact, the man was thought to be mildly demented; and so, by some sure popular instinct, everyone called him "Professor."

It was with no idea of fashioning myself upon this eccentric model of a man that I went to college. Nor yet was it with any particular profession in view; for I recall that nothing used to annoy me more than to have some respectable friend of the family inquire: "And what does the young man expect to do when he gets through college?" I rather hoped not to have to do anything; and if my parents did not share this hope, they were at least convinced, apart from any question of vocation, of the great advantage of possessing a "good education." I went to college, therefore, somewhat as a matter of course; not, certainly, to become a professor, but to obtain a good education. Whether this object was attained or not, the four years in college was to me a wonderful adventure in the wide world of the human spirit, an adventure which at the time seemed well worth while, quite apart from any question of its practical application. In this idea, I was greatly encouraged by certain professors who seemed greatly interested in my adventure, encouraging it for all they were worth. And these men had an insidious fascination for me because, contrary to all I had supposed, they were not mere road guides, uninterested in the country because they knew it by heart, mechanically directing travellers as part of the day's work, and collecting a fee for services rendered; but, like the several Knights in the *Faerie Queene*, were themselves impelled by some inner demon to venture beyond the beaten paths, scarcely knowing whither they were going or what they might find, but pursuing still, seemingly interested rather in the search itself than in the end of it. And so they welcomed

me, content that I should seek for something even if I found it not. What I should seek, or where I might find it, they never told me; but by subtle suggestion, and still subtler example, contrived to give to my quest a certain direction.

It is impertinent to this sad tale to describe the many interesting countries into which my adventure took me: as, for example, the country of Philosophy, into which so many well defined but long since abandoned roads led, all taking different directions but coming out at the same place, the place called Nowhere, in which many people serenely sat doing nothing in particular; or that other and quite different country of History, where there were only innumerable, intricately threaded faint paths, leading to the place called Everywhere, in which were all sorts of people busily engaged in doing nothing in general. Suffice it to say that the four years were up before I had more than begun to get the lay of the land. Less than ever did I desire to return to the known world and tread in monotonous routine the dusty streets of Now and Here. How fine, I thought, to remain always in this unknown country! How fine not to have "to do" anything! And one day it dawned upon me that this was precisely the case of my admired professors. Here they were, confined for life in this delightful country of the mind, with nothing "to do," privileged to go on as best they could with the great adventure. From that moment I was a lost man. I was bound to become a professor.

II

By great good luck and much plodding industry this honorable distinction was attained in due course. In the

process of attaining it, doubtless much of the glamor that in youthful student days had hung mistily about the position was inevitably dispelled. And yet I was greatly content with my bargain. Fortune had happily placed me in an agreeable corner of the world; and I reflected, with Bishop Butler, that in a universe such as this is, inhabited by a creature such as man is, not all things are ordered as one might wish; so that in the course of some years I made those adjustments to the resistant facts of reality which most aspiring youths have to make. But all this is nothing to the point, except to say that it was during these years, and as a part of this adjustment, that I became aware of two profound truths; truths which were obvious enough indeed, but to which I had hitherto given but slight attention.

It need not be said that professors are an extremely impractical people; absent minded, as even the comic papers have found out, continually occupied with profound excogitations, and inclined, therefore, to take the world, and their place in it, very much for granted. Thus it happened that in our university one of the profound truths to which I have referred would probably not have been noticed by any member of the faculty, had it not been so often explained by the president, and with earnestness and eloquence elucidated at commencement time, and on other festival occasions, when noted local statesmen, successful business men, and pedagogical experts were found willing to turn aside from the pressing duties of real life to consider for a brief hour the fundamental problems of higher education. The truth which was thus so often elaborated, I cannot pretend to phrase as happily as I have often heard it phrased; but what I understood these clever men to say was that the state paid me a salary for which

some equivalent might reasonably be expected in return.

By the nature of their duties being often required to give long and profound consideration to matters of no great importance, professors are more disposed than other men to meditate at leisure those ideas of vital significance which occasionally come their way. This new idea I therefore looked at for a long time from every point of view. That the state paid me a salary, could not be denied; that some equivalent might reasonably be expected in return appeared to be, the more I turned it over, an eminently just conclusion. From the first the proposition as a whole won my complete assent; and my attention was chiefly occupied with some of its more obscure implications; as, for example, was I by any chance already rendering any service in return for my salary? If so, was the salary equal to the service rendered? Should the work of a professor be of a nature, or should it not be of a nature, to be easily measured in terms of money? And in either case what was that work? These questions gave me much concern. At best, certainly, the professor's salary could not be regarded as princely. Did not someone once say that professors, of all able men the most poorly paid, might all be making a great deal of money had they not chosen to renounce the lower for the higher life? I must confess that this attractive idea, to which I sometimes timidly assented, did not in the end prove altogether convincing, and it had besides the disadvantage of not being relevant. It did not alter the fact that I was not a lawyer, or a captain of industry, or a plumber, but a professor; one of those, if you will, who had voluntarily renounced the pursuit of gain; and having done so it seemed to me that I must perforce face the practical question of what was the service, if any, which I

rendered for the salary, such as it was, which the state did unquestionably pay over to me.

Much light was shed on these perplexing problems by that other profound truth which was explained to us, with rather more elaboration than the first, by the free spirits of the uncloistered outside world. We were assured that, whereas the knowledge acquired by students from learned professors was an excellent thing in itself, and even a necessary part of a liberal education, it still remained true, inasmuch as this knowledge would inevitably slip from the mind after a time, that the chief value of four years in college was not so much the result of any mere book learning as it was of the daily contact with men and affairs outside the class room. The college career, rather than the college course, was the thing: the friendships formed in chapter house and boarding club, the experience gained on the campus and the athletic field, all the varied activities of the four fruitful years spent on this mimic stage of the world,—these would prove of chief value in real life; and it was the fond memory of these activities that would remain with the alumnus, returning after many years to his alma mater, to remind him of his membership in the company of the liberally educated.

This idea, even the first time I heard it presented, did not, somehow or other, strike me as altogether novel. Many students seemed often so much more alert in conducting an election than in writing an essay, appeared so much more intelligent in discussing gridiron conflicts than in describing the Wars of Religion, and in general took their class work with such settled even if commendable resignation, that I had sometimes wondered whether they did not learn more from each other than from the faculty.

Not that the students, I imagined, were more to blame than their instructors. The average man does not hunger and thirst after knowledge any more than after righteousness. The writing of an essay, when everything is said, is a task like any other. The Wars of Religion are dull enough in all conscience. And if it be true, as I have heard said, that the born teacher is one who each day "sets his students' imagination aflame," I had to confess that the born teacher is very rare. Of course I took the conventional, academic view that the situation, whoever was to blame for it, was one to be deplored, and corrected if possible. Like the British House of Commons on a famous occasion, I often highly resolved that the evil had increased, was increasing, and ought to be diminished, without seeing very clearly how that desired end might be attained. It was very consoling, therefore, to learn that there was no call to be distressed, that the situation, on the whole, was quite as it should be. I was reminded of the well known epigram which has it that Harvard would be a great university if it were not for the students; and I wondered if it would not be more modern to say that Harvard, or Kansas, would be a great university if it were not for the professors.

Personally, I thought it would be perplexing indeed if it should turn out so; and I was more than ever concerned to know what it was that a professor, paid by the state, had to do with these young people, so terribly at ease in Zion, who in increasing numbers assembled every year at the university to educate themselves. How many of them came to college, and how many were only sent? They seemed not to be in any sense a picked or chosen company. They were Everybody's children, who often replied, when I casually asked them why they came to college, that they

"just came"; and who sometimes asked me in return if it was not a good place to come to. I could not deny it, I who had gone to college without knowing why. Sometimes I passed them in review, as it were, searching for those of whom one could say, "the university is a bad place for you." There were those aspiring youths who could not decide in what branch of human learning they preferred to specialize, and with irresolution drifted from mathematics to history, from history to sociology, and so on to journalism. There were the engaging, well set up chaps, ambitious to be thought men of the world, who were willing, without fear and without research, to take on a little general culture, but who seemed to think it not quite good form to know anything for certain. There were the more serious youths who deeply pondered the problem of existence. Very modern in their ideas of Social Service, wishing not to be thought irreligious although not subscribing to any formal creed, they appeared to enjoy a high sense of having reconciled all the antinomies, inasmuch as they willingly accepted, with certain reservations, the doctrine of evolution, and yet found it not inconsistent to be present at meetings designed to promote the cause of true Christianity through the discussion of "Jesus Christ as Head Coach," or other up to date and opportune topics. No, I could not deny that, for all of these, the university was a good place to be. Least of all, perhaps, could I deny it in the case of that multitude of trim-frocked young women, bubbling over with health and the joy of living, who invaded and seemed to possess the university; who so obviously found it a good place to be; so excellent a place in which to be initiated into literature and the fine arts, into history and the social sciences, and into a sorority; those

devotees of fashion and the higher life who were equally chagrined at failing to receive a high grade or an invitation to the party, who attended classes so regularly, took notes so assiduously, and were often able to reply so neatly to every sort of question—of which they had learned the answer.

For all of these excellent children, whom one never expected to step out of the beaten path or peep over the edge of a conventional idea, the university was at least not a bad place in which to be. But then what of the illustrious minority, the saving remnant of young men and women who were not content to skirt the outer edge of the intellectual country? A few there were always with the genuine curiosity of the scholar; a few who wished not merely to seek wisdom but to pursue it as well. To all such I confess I was ever partial, delighted to find them interested in knowledge for its own sake rather than for the sake of a grade. I never knowingly did anything to discourage their fondness for useless ideas, or to check the instinctive aptitude which they sometimes exhibited for every kind of heresy. These were the pupils whose imagination the born teacher might each day set aflame. These were the pupils who would go far if the pace was properly set. But in that case the others, left far behind without a guide, would be in danger of altogether losing their way. Here they were then, pellmell, Everybody's children in Everybody's university; and the professor, comfortably drawing his salary month by month, had to decide whether he could best serve the state by attending mainly to the great majority or by attending mainly to the saving remnant. The professor had to decide whether he would endeavor to make

the university a school of higher education or merely a higher school of education.

The answer to this question I found by no means easy. In a community saturated with the sentiment of democracy it might seem to go without saying that if the people wished to maintain a great public playground where a little useful information, neither dangerous nor too esoteric, could be picked up by the way, the paid professor was there to give them what they wanted. And yet, in this community whose democracy was touched with idealism, it seemed reasonable to suppose that intelligent people who sent their children to the university would desire for them the higher education in some serious sense. At least I could not think that the "Old Grad," even if he did customarily discourse longer on football than on Latin, really supposed that the university was maintained at great expense primarily for the practice of the new dances or the cultivation of college spirit. I came therefore to the conclusion, without being very sure of its being the right one, that the professor might safely concern himself with the intellectual interests rather than with "student interests," and with a good conscience give his best efforts to those pupils (a considerable number after all, if one allowed for the natural conservatism of the normal young fellows who wish not to appear conspicuous) who were capable of serious intellectual effort, allowing the others to come and go, without too rigid inquiry into their attainments, on the assumption that four years in college could not, on almost any terms, do them any great harm.

In this opinion I long continued, and should doubtless have persisted to this day, had it not been for a new order

of ideas which began to make its way into the quiet academic world. It must have been about the year 1910, or
some such inconvenient date, that I began to have an un-
easy sense of things gone wrong; and I was shortly made
aware that the question had not to do with the students
but with me; the real question was not whether I should
concern myself with serious intellectual interests, but
whether the intellectual interests with which I had so long
concerned myself were in fact serious. Let the professor
work his students as much as he liked; it was still pertinent, I found, to ask of what practical benefit was all this
endeavor. I had considered the whole question from the
point of view of the efficiency of the students, and all this
it now turned out was a great mistake; what I should in
fact have asked was whether the professor himself was
efficient.

Like the good John Bunyan, I was now much "tumbled
up and down in my mind." As soon as I felt the edge of
that word efficiency, I knew there was sharp work to be
done. A word so self-contained, yet so little restful; a word
so keen and precise; a word so firm and metallic, so hard
and yet so resilient, would surely cut straight and ruthlessly through all that was vague and uncertain in the
world, would prick every bubble of speculative thinking,
expose all soft idealisms, and open up those obscure and
shaded nooks of the human mind where emotion keeps its
day, and energy is dissipated in the vain striving after
impossible things. Suddenly confronted with this uncompromising word, there was little I could set down in ex-
tenuation. All the vague adumbrations of ideas with
which I had puffed up my soul in vanity, weighed in the
balance against this word, were found but trifles light as

air. There was nothing for it but to surrender at discretion; to begin life over; to find out, first of all, what efficient education was like, and then what I might do in the way of promoting it.

III

Left to myself I should most probably have gone wrong. Fortunately, I was not left to myself. A great number of disquisitions, on efficiency in general and on educational efficiency in particular, exposed the theory of the thing; while certain changes in the traditional college curriculum, changes which, unperceived by me, had been going on for many years, furnished examples of its practical application. Instructed in theory and fortified by concrete illustration, I soon learned to detect the efficiency expert, or any fair specimen of his work, entirely unaided, and with what seemed to me a commendable degree of precision. My success in this matter was doubtless due to the habit of employing, out of many tests, three principal ones, which it was said should be applied to determine the efficiency of every sort of activity. These tests may be conveniently put in the form of questions; so that one is always on the right track in asking, of any educational institution or course of study, whether it has a practical value, whether it has a measurable value, and whether its value is equal to its cost. I must confess that for a long time the whole business was a purely empirical process on my part; but in time I came to see that these three excellent tests, far from being mere arbitrary rules of thumb, were all clearly derived from a single fundamental principle, a principle which had the advantage of being

grounded in revelation as well as in reason, the principle, namely, that education has to do primarily with the things that are seen and temporal rather than with the things that are unseen and eternal.

That this way of regarding the matter had so long escaped me is perhaps not so inexplicable as one would suppose. My failure was doubtless due to excessive preoccupation with the dead past. As a student of history I had been much impressed with a distinction, over subtle no doubt, which old Martin Luther, and Socrates before him, attempted to draw between the inner or spiritual man and the outer or temporal man. Men whom the world had fallen into the habit of calling great had made so much of this distinction that I also, being somewhat conventionally minded, came to regard it as of great importance. From all I could learn, I imagined that if history had any meaning, if the study of the past revealed anything which we could safely speak of as "progress" or "development," it was to be found precisely in this painfully won, even if inadequate, separation of the inner from the outer man, and in the subordination, as yet only partially effective to be sure, of material to spiritual values. Such limited experience as I had had, confirmed by the opinions of reputed wise men in all ages, led me to suppose that spiritual and material values were of a different order altogether, and that the former could neither be fostered nor measured by means that were appropriate to the latter. Preoccupied with these not very precise ideas, I suppose it never occurred to me to ask whether schools and churches, or the intellectual activities which seem always in some fashion connected with them, were efficient, or whether they were worth all they cost. I had rather thought of such

institutions and activities as devoted to fostering those ideal interests which humanity seemed to find indispensable; as devoted to preserving and promoting, certainly never as effectively as could be wished, that indefinable thing called wisdom or virtue, which, as Socrates said, is "surely the one true coin for which all things should be exchanged."

Now, it had required no little courage to engage in the business of education on these terms. Strive as one might, profits were small, exceeding slow in the realization, and sometimes, even with the closest figuring, seemed to have altogether vanished. How elusive and intangible a thing was this wisdom, or liberal culture, in the service of which so many buildings were erected, so many salaries paid, so many unread books printed! As of old it could doubtless still be said that "wisdom crieth aloud, she uttereth her voice in the streets"; but though she might speak with the tongues of angels her message seemed too often all but lost in the noises of the forum or the market place. Where then was the professor to maintain that he had promoted understanding, or done effective battle against the plangent platitude or the pretentious humbug? Who could claim to demonstrate beyond peradventure that right reason followed in the wake of Latin composition, or that much study of history fostered the righteousness that exalteth a nation? On these terms it was difficult indeed for the professor to maintain his own worth, by his works to prove to the eye of sense that he was anything more than a late survival, a kind of tradition, as it were, which men repeat still, well aware that it has but a poetic significance.

With what relief then, with what a sense of assured results, might not the professor turn to a theory of education

which, identifying the inner with the outer man, concerned itself with material and measurable realities! Now it was that I first fully grasped the profound significance of a saying of Pascal. "How rightly," he says, "do men judge by external rather than by internal standards. Which of us two shall enter first? The most able? But I am as able as he: we should have to fight about that. He has four footmen, while I have but one. That is something which can be seen. There is nothing to do but to count. It is clearly my place to yield, and I am a fool if I contest it. Thus we remain at peace, the greatest of all possible blessings." Applying this qualitative arithmetic, I found all the great problems of education much simplified, and placed in the way of an easy solution. One had only to count, an extremely easy thing to do, and very precise in its results. One had but to count the students in all the universities to determine which was the greatest university, the enrollment in all the courses to determine which was the best course. That student was the most liberally educated who obtained the best paying job. The ablest professor was the one who accumulated the most degrees, or printed the most books; while the most efficient was he who taught most hours in the day, or whose name was attended with the longest retinue of varied and noted activities.

"He has four footmen, while I have but one." But why indeed should he have four since I have but one? Let us each have two, a very good number for any man, so that we may go in together, thus banishing jealousy and contention from the world. If this solution did not occur to Pascal, it was doubtless because he lived in an aristocratic age. But in our day it is difficult to imagine any other, or to conceive why it should not be applied to those institu-

tions which, being supported by public taxation, are necessarily devoted to the promotion of equality. It seemed clear, therefore, that the efficiency of a university should be judged, not alone by the number of its activities, but also by the uniformity of its results. Formerly I had supposed this altogether impracticable; I now came to see that it was within the range of the possible. Organization and system, excellent and obtainable substitutes for inspiration, would do the business in the end. The university had in fact to be standardized. Let it but be provided with a sufficiently elaborated mechanism of co-ordinated and intricately reticulated compulsory and restrictive rules and regulations, and one could not doubt that professors would be made efficient in spite of themselves, or that students would become educated by passive resistance to an established routine. If all professors conducted their classes by the same method, and applied the same method in testing the attainments of their students; if no professor devoted more or less time than every other to supervising the work of his classes, if none made that work either more or less interesting, or failed to observe the rule requiring that a just percentage of his pupils should attain excellence in the end; why, in that case, one might look forward to the happy day when students would enter the Latin course as readily as the course in Oral Expression, being assured beforehand that the chances of achieving the mental quality stamped Grade A would be precisely the same in the one course as in the other.

Excellent results such as these could not of course be obtained without excellent men. I was therefore well aware that for the standardization of the university a new type of men was needed: alert and active men, practical,

hustling fellows, live wires; a different sort altogether from the traditional professor, hall-marked by a timid and casual air, over much given to "dreams and the reading of many books, in which are also divers vanities," as the Preacher says. But I had only to look around me to realize that the new professor was already on the ground. Everywhere there appeared to be an increasing number of efficiency experts: systematizers and methodologists, pedagogical statisticians, instructors who gave the impression of having reduced the art of teaching to the level of an exact science. Nor could I doubt that the New Professor was not only known but justified of his works. He everywhere brought with him new life and a sense of lifted horizons, so that the task of disciplining the minds of students, and of fitting them at once for social service and a well paid job, seemed the least part of the professor's duties. I wonder now that any one could have thought to justify an expensive university so long as it aimed only to shape the thought and conduct of the rising generation! The New Professor taught us that the campus must be made coextensive with the commonwealth. Brought into contact with all the people, conferring upon them those material benefits which could be exactly measured, and once felt could not be forgot, the university would win their undivided allegiance, and would at last become, what its founders intended it to be, the palladium of all our liberties.

One could not long remain cold in the presence of such a splendid ideal as this; nor long refuse one's sympathy to the men who were engaged in providing the highly articulated organization which was necessary to attain it. I had long been sceptical of the possibility of advancing educa-

tion through the multiplication of administrative devices; was doubtless a little repelled by the New Professor's complacent confidence in the efficacy of so much machinery; a little jealous, perhaps, on account of the instant applause with which his proposals were greeted by the many. And yet there was a compelling fascination about these men. The New Professor conducted himself with such a busy air of industry and of things accomplished; he spread about in the quiet academic world so bright a sense of precision and practicality and of workable mechanisms; he was so alertly on the job, foreseeing every difficulty only to dispose of it by a new device; was so earnestly methodical and so methodically earnest; was so furnished forth with profound and brightly furbished convictions, even about little things; and in general was so persistently up to the mark doing his level best, and sometimes a second best, in the search for a perfect educational Schematism, that one could by no means refuse him a great admiration.

Admire him or not, I realized that the New Professor had come to stay. He was a part of the *Zeitgeist,* which it is useless to resist however little one may enjoy it. I recognized the New Professor as an embodiment of the *Zeitgeist* as soon as I realized that it was his foreordained mission to bring education into harmony with the main trend of thought in society at large. "The Jesuit," says Mr. Irving Babbitt, "unduly encouraged the individual in the hope that he might cast off the burden of his sin upon the priest"; and I have his word for it, although he is doubtless too little in sympathy with popular ideas to be a good judge, that the underlying notion of the present day humanitarianism is to think, likewise, that the individual may "cast off his burden upon society." Doubtless no one

has better expressed this fruitful idea than Rousseau:
"Men are naturally good," he said; "it is society that
corrupts them." Now I had always thought of Rousseau,
taking credit to himself for all his virtues while laying
all his vices to the account of his neighbors, as having
invented a most easy solution for all our social problems.
What could be happier, then, than to apply this philosophy, everywhere so popular in the world at large, to the
miniature world of the university? And this, it seemed to
me, was precisely what the New Professor was up to:
devising the perfect organization as a substitute for personal responsibility, thus enabling the student, and the
professor too, rest his soul, to cast off the burden of education upon a vicariously mediating institution.

It was not difficult to foresee that our pupils, with the
enthusiasm of youth, would readily adapt themselves to a
philosophy of this sort. Occupied with many things, they
would inevitably find inspection of the formal record
much easier than self-examination as a test of excellence.
Matters would be much simplified if students, delegating
the business of studying certain subjects to professors of
established reputation, could take their education for
granted as soon as they had obtained the credits necessary
for a degree; if none could question their religion so long
as they were down on the Registrar's books as having declared a preference for some or other denomination of
professing Christians; if none could object to their conduct so long as they observed the rules laid down by the
committee on social affairs. And if some failed, even on
these terms, it was a great advantage to know that the fault
was in the system and not in themselves. A recent contrib-
utor to the *Outlook* has described his own case, which was

precisely of this sort, with admirable insight. At his university, he said, the professors were not inspiring, many student activities distracted his attention, an inequitable system of grading discouraged him, and in general the atmosphere of the place was not conducive to interest in serious things: for all these reasons he had "lost the capacity for work."

No one can deny that the young man had a just grievance; for it is a serious thing, in this busy world, to lose the capacity for work, and certainly an institution lacked efficiency in which four years' residence could give that result. On the other hand, it is right to point out that we have only recently begun to standardize our universities; and in matters of this sort not everything can be accomplished in the twinkling of an eye. Already, in the mere recognition that our fortune is in our stars not in ourselves, we have undoubtedly taken a long step forward. It remains only to define wisdom and virtue with complete elaboration in terms of the average social judgment. Then any student, or professor either, even the most indifferent, may lie down in the lap of the university in the confident expectation of being nursed into the achievement of something excellent.

IV

It must be confessed that we are still far from having attained this desirable condition, even in the middle west, which is well known to be a most progressive and enterprising community. Yet the movement is well under way; so well under way that I myself regard it, with admiration indeed, but with a certain resignation, as one who

already thinks of himself as belonging to an older generation. I think it a great point in my favor that I clearly
foresaw the passing of the old order, and that I did my best
to adapt myself to the new. I tried desperately, for a long
time, to acquire a new stock of ideals, to banish useless
dreams, to take on at least such an appearance of efficiency
as might enable me, under favorable circumstances, to
pass muster before an inspector from the Carnegie Institution. It cannot be said that I achieved any great success.
Doubtless I had been too long habituated to an older
order of ideas; and it is well known that defects in early
training, extremely difficult to overcome in later life, are
likely to discount whatever native talent one may possess.
Every year, therefore, I find myself falling farther and
farther behind, relatively. It may be that I am more
efficient than I was; but, compared with the truly competent, I know well that I am at best nothing more than
"something just as good" as the genuine.

Sometimes I yield to the insidious temptation which
induces a defeated man to disparage the merits of the
victor, that he may regard his own defects as a finer kind
of virtue. Is it perhaps after all true, I say to myself, that
the more efficient education becomes, the less efficient become the educated? Is it true that spiritual benefits can be
so precisely noted and set down in terms of material value?
Perhaps, after all?—And so I deceive myself at times with
formulating a kind of slave morality, well suited to flatter
the vanity of one who has succumbed, in some measure,
to men of super qualities. 'Tis but a harmless delusion! I
know it well; and am resigned, on the whole, to the notion
that I shall never be an efficient professor in a completely
standardized university. I will do what I can, but hope to

keep close in my sheltered corner, and to avoid, if possible, the Survey and the Questionnaire, well aware that they would expose all my counterfeit values to the curious inspection of an unsympathetic world. Already I remind myself, and in the future I doubt not I shall remind myself more and more, of the old "Professor" in shiny frock coat who came every Spring to prepare our fire wood. Like him I may, figuratively speaking, make a good living sawing wood; but like him also I foresee myself still nourishing certain fantastic ideas which the sympathetic will regard as harmless eccentricities, and the unfriendly as dangerous heresies. Such is the irony of fate!—that I should come to resemble the Old Professor whom in my youth I thought so little admirable! As yet, it is true, I do not habitually wear a frock coat; but I console myself with the thought that everything comes to him who waits.

Learning and Teaching

THE profession of teaching is universally regarded as a necessary occupation. Since the colleges and universities are filled with young people eager to learn, it is taken for granted that there must be no end of instructors and professors eager to teach them. And so the words learning and teaching commonly go coupled and inseparable. Nevertheless, I should like to dissociate these two words and throw away one of them. Learning I think excellent. I have always been (I hope) a learner, and I hope I always shall be. But I have never desired to teach any one anything, and I dislike extremely to be called a teacher. I have an aversion to teaching and teachers.*

No doubt there is among you a disciple of Freud eager to explain that this aversion springs from some infantile experience. He is right, and I gladly furnish him with the circumstances essential to the explanation. I can still vividly recall the sight of many overworked mothers, standing, gingham-aproned, at kitchen doors perhaps, looking severely out at the elusive Johnny or Katie. I can

* An essay first published in *Cornell Contemporary*, II (Oct. 24, 1930), 13–14.

still vividly recall the tired, stringent voice: "You, Johnny, come back here this minute. If you do that once more I'll teach you! I'll smack you good." Another scene comes to mind. A dingy room, filled with chalk dust and bored small children sitting imprisoned behind battered desks clamped to the floor. A boy raises his hand: "Please, teacher, can I get a drink?" "No, Billy, you *may* not. You've just had a drink. You must be quiet and learn your lesson."

The Freudian psychologist now knows the origin of my aversion to teaching and teachers. Since the aversion persisted, of course, I have had to rationalize it. That has not been difficult to do. It seems to me obvious that when Johnny enters the spacious portals of the high school or of the university he encounters there (under whatever camouflage of pleasant metaphors and dignified ritual) the same fundamental conception of teaching, and much the same attitude in teachers, that prevailed in the backyard and the grade school. As an entering freshman in college, for example, he in effect says to the authorities: "I have come to college to be educated. What are you going to do about it?" In effect the authorities reply: "We are going to do a great deal about it—everything in fact. On Mondays, Wednesdays and Fridays you will go at 9 o'clock to room A, and at 10 o'clock to room B, where you will find professors X and Y who will respectively teach you physics and history. They will tell you daily what chapter to read in what book, what themes to write, and on what subjects. On Tuesdays, Thursdays and Saturdays other professors will likewise teach you French, psychology and hygiene. If you do what each professor tells you each one will give you 3 credits. When you have accumulated 120

credits the college authorities will give you a degree. Thus for four years your esteemed professors, aided by a most elaborate set of administrative devices, will teach you how to behave. If you fail to behave properly, they will smack you good—they will refuse to give you a degree."

In a somewhat milder form, this process of teaching continues through the graduate school. The pupil is habituated to it, and so is the professor. The candidate says: "I wish to become a scholar. What must I do?" The Dean replies: "You must in that case obtain a higher degree—a Ph.D. In order to do that you must pass X number of advanced courses, totalling Y number of credits. That is, you must do more of what you did in college, only you must do it under aggravated pressure. But above all you must write a thesis under the direction of some professor." "What must I write about?" "The professor under whose direction you write it will tell you all about that." Perhaps the subject of the thesis turns out to be, "The Longitudinal Vibrations of a Rubbed String," or, "The Genesis of the Kansas-Nebraska Act." Very good subjects they are too, since the experienced professor has himself selected them. And very well treated they may be, and often are, since the professor is likely to direct and supervise, at every step, the writing of the thesis. If the student does what the professor tells him to do (especially if he writes his thesis as nearly as possible as the professor himself might have written it) he will undoubtedly, in due course, obtain his degree, he will become a scholar. Usually the student does his best to behave as he is taught to behave. He does his best not to disappoint the professor, because, you see, he doesn't want to be smacked good—he doesn't want to miss his degree.

Up to this point the process of teaching and learning is called education. But when Johnny leaves the university for "real life" his education is by no means finished. The process of teaching continues under other names. He will always find plenty of people to teach him to behave, and to smack him good if he needs it. There is, for example, the government, which in the last four hundred years has gradually supplanted the Church as the Great Teacher of conduct and morals. And I scarcely need mention the innumerable self-constituted associations of public-spirited citizens that exist for the purpose of teaching us all how to do one good act each day, and to refrain from doing any bad act.

In justice to teachers, as well as to myself, I ought to say that my aversion is not really to teaching, but to mis-applied teaching and to overzealous teachers. There are indeed many things that may properly be taught. You may properly teach a dog to do tricks, or a horse to work in harness. You may properly teach children to dress them-selves and to behave mannerly at table. You may properly teach boys and girls to add and subtract, to use a slide rule, to drive an automobile, to run a lathe, to read music or to pronounce English or French words correctly, to use chemicals without blowing up the laboratory, to test the genuineness of handwriting or the authenticity of his-torical documents. There are a thousand things that may and should be taught, and the teaching of such things is a useful art. Generally speaking, you may properly teach any subject in so far as it has a definite factual content or a special technique to be mastered. Some part of most subjects studied in college and university may therefore be taught. Of mathematics, physics, chemistry and the

biological sciences there is a great deal that may be taught.
Of history, literature, philosophy, economics, and the
like, there is much less, but still something. What may be
taught of any subject is that body of specific information
which, possessed by one person, can be communicated to,
and made use of unchanged by another. But the purpose
of studying most subjects in universities is not to master a
technique, but to liberalize the mind—to become possessed of insight and judgment and understanding, to
acquire that wisdom which is the fine flower of learning.
These qualities of the mind cannot be acquired through
teaching. They can neither be cribbed from books, nor
borrowed from professors, nor purchased from an institution. They can be acquired by any person only through
his own efforts (stimulated and directed by professors as
you please), and in the measure that his opportunities, his
industry, his curiosity and his intelligence make possible.
In short, they can be acquired only by learning.

The misapplied teaching which tends to destroy learning, to degrade it to the level of passive acceptance of pre-
digested facts and ready-made ideas, is no doubt a function
of democracy. As such, in spite of my aversion to it, I can
see that it has its practical uses. Its virtue is to enable the
many to be easily directed and conveniently labeled; and
in this mechanical and democratic age it is easier to deal
with people, as with things, if they are standardized and
neatly classified. A degree is a proper label of a standardized product. It serves to classify the holder. After all a
college man is a college man the country over, known on
mere inspection of his trademark to be eligible for admis-
sion to a university club. I would not abolish labels. It
would distress too many people to be without them. But I

think that college men might be labeled with much less expense, delay, and travail of spirit than is necessary under the present system of teaching. I have thought of a much simpler system. Maybe there are other and better ones, but I have not heard of them. My plan is this. I would confer on each freshman, as soon as he had presented proper credentials and had paid his full tuition, the desired degree. Nothing further would be required of him. Needing no credits, he would not need to attend classes. If he had no intellectual interests he could go home, or devote himself wholly to what are now called rightly enough "student interests." Such students as might be interested in learning would be free to remain and engage in it, with the help of such professors, no doubt always a sufficient number, as might be willing to assist them.

Such a plan would have many real advantages. For one thing it would facilitate the purchase of a degree, and at the same time make an honest business of it. But its chief advantage would be the removal of many obstacles to learning. There would be no artificial incentive to teach, since nothing could be gained by it. Half the instructors, and more than half the students, being free to do as they pleased, would not know what to do, and would end by going away. With the faculty and the student body so greatly reduced, the funds and the equipment of the university would be more than adequate to the needs of those who persisted, in spite of all dissuasion, in the pursuit of knowledge. Since no requirements would be made of any one, all the complicated administrative machinery could be dismantled. Deans would cease to function. Their offices would be closed, and their treasured records and statistical graphs could be carted away, or left to serve the

useful purpose of gathering dust. Faculty meetings and standing committees would cease from troubling. Publicity departments, the *Alumni News,* and self-constituted organizations for annoying the Old Grads could be mercifully discontinued. A few trustees would be sufficient to guard the funds and invest them wisely. The president, being no longer saddled with the duties of a politician and promoter, might be selected for his attainments as a scholar rather than for his reputation as an educator. In short, many advantages, all of which might be included in one; the university could cease to be an institution, partly commercial and partly penal, and become quite simply a place of learning.

The Art of Writing

I REALIZE that it is presumptuous for me, a professor of history, to speak on the art of writing to an audience in which are present professors of English who have devoted their lives to the theory and practice of that art. My excuse is that I am not addressing them. They should not be here; but since they are here I hasten to reassure them. I shall not raise any of those friendship-breaking questions which only experts like themselves are competent to answer. For example, is it sometimes permissible to deliberately split an infinitive? Or does an infinitive, when split, invariably writhe in agony and die among its worshippers? Or again, is a preposition something which may never, under any circumstances, be used to end a sentence with? These and all questions of similar import I shall carefully avoid. It is understood, then, that in discussing the art of writing I do not claim to speak as one having authority. I merely give my personal impressions for what they are worth; and if they are worth anything at all it is only because the art of writing, endured always as a malady rather than adopted as a racket, has been the most persistent and absorbing interest of my life.*

* An address given at Smith College early in 1942; printed by

121

With the writer's malady I was infected at the early age
of eleven. Why I should have been susceptible to it is
something of a mystery, for at that time I had never read
a book, or had a book read to me, or heard any one talk
about books or literature or the art of writing. What carried the infection, however, I remember very clearly. At
the age of eleven there fell into my hands, through the
agency, curiously enough, of that unliterary institution,
the public school, a sample copy of *Saturday Night*—a
weekly journal devoted exclusively to serials (then called
continued stories) of the adventure, western, detective
type. Of one of these stories I read the first installment, not
knowing until too late that it was only the first installment.
Imagine then my despair when, having followed with
breathless interest the fortunes of the lovely heroine until,
stalked by the implacable villain to a lonely and deserted
house, she was menaced by the fate that is worse than death
—imagine my despair when, at this dramatic crisis in the
story, I was confronted with those bleak, uncompromising
words, in parenthesis, "To be continued in our next." I
was stunned. I said in effect, they can't do this to me. It
appeared that they could. When I asked for five cents for
the next issue of *Saturday Night,* my mother, never brutal
till then, said no, you mustn't read such stories, they are
not good reading. It was then I first learned that important
distinction between good literature and stories that are
interesting to read. I did not want good literature. I
wanted, more than anything else in life, the next issue of
Saturday Night. Quite apart from the story, there was
something about the journal itself—some magic in the

---

permission of the Cornell University Library. An earlier version
was given at Wells College, Oct. 8, 1941.

garish title, blackly spread across the page, something in the feel and smell of the cheap, soft, dampish paper—that had for me the essential glamor of romance. From that moment my purpose in life was clear. I would be an author, a writer of stories for *Saturday Night*.

The desire to be a writer gave me an interest in reading. Unfortunately, *Saturday Night* was barred, and since the best was not available I had to be satisfied with the less good. The less good was to be found in the public library, a small collection of books got together by some public-spirited ladies of the town, and open twice a week to those who paid twenty-five cents a quarter. Somehow I obtained twenty-five cents, and in this immense collection of perhaps five hundred volumes I spent many hours, and from it took out and read many books, ranging from Greek mythology to *Eric the Red*. One day I saw on the shelf a volume bound in plain green cloth, with strange foreign looking words on the back—"Anna Karenina. Tolstoy." I took it down and read the opening sentence: "All happy families are happy in the same way; each unhappy family has its own way of being unhappy." Not bad, I thought. Perhaps he has something there. I took the volume to the desk, and asked the gray-haired, friendly lady: "Is this a good book?" The lady glanced at the title, then looked at me, over her spectacles, searchingly sizing me up, no doubt wondering whether, for a boy of perhaps thirteen, *Anna Karenina* was after all quite the thing. At last she said: "It's a very powerful book." Nothing else—a wise lady I've always thought. I said: "I'll take it." And so I took *Anna Karenina* home, and read it by the light of the kerosene lamp, sitting in the old tall-backed rocking chair, with my feet on the fender of the simmering base burner.

Not knowing that it was good literature, I found it interesting. This is pretty good, I thought; nearly, if not
quite, as good as the stories in *Saturday Night*. It was the
first independent critical literary judgment I ever pronounced.

In high school something more was added to my knowledge and sophistication. There was a teacher, with some
experience of life, and an unusual knowledge of good
literature. Every day she copied on the blackboard, and
had us learn, some famous quotation—"Who steals my
purse steals trash"—"To thine own self be true," and the
like. From her I learned much about good literature, and
something about the rudiments of English grammar—as,
for example, that "He has went" is not, strictly speaking,
the preferred form. And so it happened that when I
entered the university, having read a good deal but nothing systematically, I was more determined than ever to
be a writer, preferably a writer of novels. But not novels
of the sort that appeared in *Saturday Night,* since these,
as I now knew, were not good literature. The novels I
would write would be good literature—as good as *Anna
Karenina,* or even, if fortune was favorable, as good as
Ben Hur or the *Last Days of Pompeii.*

It was inevitable then that, as a freshman bound to be
a writer of good literature, the course in English composition, or Rhetoric as it was then called, should interest
me more than any other. The text was Genung's *Rhetoric*
—not at all a bad book—which I read and studied with
great interest. Since it was the prescribed text, there was
nothing really reprehensible in that. But I did more. I
took from the library and read with equal care all the
other Rhetorics to be found there—a feat which I like to

think must be unique in the experience of college freshmen. I read them all with care; but I was vaguely aware
that they did not after all help me very much. It was not
until much later that I understood why. The Rhetorics did
not help me much because to the unformulated question I
asked them they gave no answer. What I really asked the
Rhetorics was, "What must one do in order to learn to
write well?" The Rhetorics all, without exception, replied: "Good writing must be clear, forceful, and elegant." I have sometimes wished that I might acquire
great wealth, and that the authors of all the old Rhetorics
would come to me and ask: "What must we do in order
to acquire great wealth?" I would reply: "Great wealth
consists in a clear title to much money, forcibly secured
in banks, and elegantly available for spending."

The truth is that the Rhetorics gave me the run
around. I asked for a method, they gave me a definition.
It would have been better, of course, if the definition had
been sound. At the time I took the definition for gospel
truth, but I have since wondered about that famous definition. Good writing, the Rhetorics said, must be clear.
I think at once of an English classic, and of what is perhaps the most famous passage in it.

> 'Twas brillig and the slithy toves
> Did gyre and gimble in the wabe;
> All mimsy were the borogoves,
> And the mome raths outgrabe.

By common consent this is good writing, but is it clear?
Not by any ordinary meaning of the term. It is clear only
if you say that all good writing is clear that clearly expresses the intention of the author. In this case the

author's intention was to achieve a humorous obscurity by writing nonsense. He had a genius for that sort of thing, so that, as one may say, he achieved obscurity with a clarity rarely if ever equaled before or since.

According to the Rhetorics good writing must be not only clear but forceful. Another passage from writing commonly accounted good comes to mind: "So we'll live, and pray, and sing, and tell old tales, and laugh at gilded butterflies, and hear poor rogues talk of court news; and we'll talk with them too. Who loses and who wins: who's in, who's out; and take upon us the mystery of things, as if we were God's spies: and we'll wear out, in a wall'd prison, packs and sects of great ones, that ebb and flow by the moon." Is this forceful? Not, I think, in the sense of the term as used by the old Rhetorics. But yes, if you mean by forceful what I mean, what any one must mean if good writing, supremely great writing, must by definition be forceful—that is to say, effective for expressing the intention of the author. Certainly no definition of good writing can be valid if it excludes, or gives the slightest ground for excluding, the poignant words of Lear to Cordelia.

Finally, according to the Rhetorics, good writing must be elegant (or beautiful, as some of them have it). Let me apply this test to a sentence in *What Price Glory?* There is a passage in which shell-shocked Lieutenant Moore, driven to hysteria by what he has seen and done, lets himself go in an effort to say what he thinks about the war. He had wondered, as his companions must often have wondered, what irony of fate it was that placed *them* in the trenches, while millions of people were safe at home, eating good food, sleeping in soft beds, and valiantly

fighting the war from arm chairs. Why were they not all in the trenches too? And now, as he shouts his incoherent denunciation of the war, the injustice of this fact strikes him with unendurable force, and he ends his tirade with a devastating indictment of the whole bloody business: "God damn every son of a bitch in the world who isn't here!" This is clear, it is past all doubt forceful; but is it elegant? The professors of Rhetoric who taught me would not, I feel sure, have thought so. But all I can say is that if all good writing must be elegant, then this is elegant; for no one will persuade me that so true and effective an expression of a profound and genuine emotion is not good writing.

The point of all this is that however you define good writing you must define your defining terms in such a way that the definition will include all good writing. Perhaps then a safer definition would be: "Good writing is writing that fully and effectively conveys the fact, the idea, or the emotion which the writer wishes to convey." Or, as Ben Franklin put it: "That is well wrote which is best adapted to obtain the object of the writer." It is all very well to define good writing, but I think that in the teaching of English composition in my day too much emphasis was placed on the definition and analysis of good writing, and too little on what the student should do in order to become a good writer. Writing is, after all an act—something that has to be done; and it is better to approach the teaching of it from the point of view of the creative processes rather than from the point of view of the created product, from the point of view of the doer rather than from the point of view of the thing done. Since my time no doubt the teaching of English composition has

been altogether reformed: but since in my time the Rhetorics did not tell me what it was necessary to do to learn to write well, I had to find out from experience as best I could; and judging from my experience there are three essential things that one must do.

The first essential is after all not something that one can do, but something that one must want to do. One must want to be a good writer. In a sense, of course, a great many people, virtually all college students, want to be able to write well, because they realize that it would be an advantage to them if they could. This wanting is sufficient to enable them to write, if not well, at least correctly. "Can one learn to write?" asks Remy de Gourmont. "If . . . the question be one of the elements of a trade, of what painters are taught in the academies, all that can indeed be learned. One can learn to write correctly, in the neutral manner. . . . One can learn to write badly, that is to say, properly, and so to merit a prize for literary excellence. One may learn to write very well, which is another way of writing very ill. How melancholy they are, those books that are well written—and nothing more!" Almost any one can learn to write correctly. A little wanting is enough for that. But if it be a question of writing really well, of attaining the something more than the correctly written, then it is first of all essential to have, in more or less acute form, what I have called the writer's malady. For one who has this malady the desire to write will be, not necessarily an exclusive interest, but at least a dominant and persistent one. This is the first essential.

If one has this first essential, the second will probably come of itself. The second essential is the inveterate habit

of reading, reading what is old as well as what is new, what is bad as well as what is good. Reading, as Bacon said, maketh the full man—full of information is what he meant. There is no harm in that. Information is a good thing for the writer as well as for any one else—if he hasn't more of it than can be readily mastered and controlled. The writer will read for information, but also with an ear always open to catch the meaning and overtones of words and the peculiar pitch and cadence of their arrangement. There will thus be deposited in the mind, in the subconscious if you prefer, an adequate vocabulary, and a sure feeling for the idioms, rhythms, and grammatical forms that are natural to the language. In time these become so much a part of the writer's mentality that he thinks in terms of them, and writes properly by ear, so to speak, rather than by rule. Thinking too precisely on the rule is apt to give to one's writing a certain correct rigidity, even a slightly archaic quality, often found in the writing of professors—particularly perhaps in the writing of those who, having unfortunately to teach English composition, are necessarily too much occupied every day with the rhetorical and grammatical innocence of college freshmen.

It is well to write correctly, but it can be overdone. Several years ago I wrote a short piece for the *Nation* in which I ventured to say: "I don't think there will be, in the near future, a general war in Europe." It was bad prophecy: and even at the time I didn't feel very sure about what I said, about the content; but it did not occur to me that the form was bad: the form seemed to me clear, forceful, and elegant enough. But not so. Within ten days a bright college girl from the wide open spaces

wrote to me as follows: "I see in the *Nation* you say: 'I don't think there will be, in the near future, a general war in Europe.' We are taught to say: 'I think there will not be, in the near future, a general war in Europe.' What about it?" What about it indeed! It was a sock in the eye for me. For three days I didn't dare write a sentence, because I couldn't remember a single rule, except that the predicate must agree with the subject, whatever that might mean. But then I recalled that Shakespeare was pretty careless about grammar, and sometimes used the word *learn* where he should have used the word *teach*. I reflected that practically all the great writers had been, first or last, caught out by the grammarians, without any effect so far as I could see, except to give them (the grammarians) a fine funeral. And so I fell back into my slovenly way of writing—"I don't think," and so on. The point is that one can't write spontaneously and well unless one can forget about the rules and depend upon the ear to save him from committing actual mayhem on the language—by writing, for example, "He has went," or "Your cordial reception has been very encouraging to Mrs W. and I." It is wide and constant reading, rather than the study of formal rhetoric, that will enable the writer to write spontaneously, and sufficiently in accord with the rules without thinking about the rules. Anyway the rules are always changing, and the best advice still is, "Be not the first by whom the new is tried, nor yet the last to lay the old aside." Wide reading will enable you to follow this rule, even if you never heard of it.

The third and most important thing to be done in order to learn to write well is to write. Never let any one persuade you to refrain from writing until you have

something to say—something important is always meant. As well tell the child to refrain from talking until he has learned to speak correctly. It is only by incessant practice in the way of gurgles and noises that he learns to speak at all; and it is only by writing much sad stuff that any one can learn to write something good enough even, as De Gourmont says, to merit a prize for literary excellence. Whether what one writes is important or not is another matter. That depends upon native intelligence and knowledge. But one thing is certain: there is no better way of developing whatever native intelligence one has, or of organizing whatever knowledge one may have acquired, than by persistently trying to put in written form what one has to say, whether important or not. Fortunately, those who are infected with the writer's malady will pay no attention to this bad advice. They will write because they must, filling pages and pages, as well aware as any one that what they write isn't important, but always hoping that in time it may be, and at all events determined to say what they find to say, whether important or not, as well as they can.

These are then the three essentials—to have an irrepressible desire to write, to be always reading with discrimination, and to be always writing as well as one can. I should like to say that the rest is silence; but you all know that a professor, once started, can't be stopped short of fifty minutes, and besides it is inconceivable that any one should discuss the art of writing without once mentioning the word *style*.

Very well. I will mention it. *Style*. How do you like it? I don't like it at all. I like it almost as little as I like the word *artistry*. I dislike the word *style* because it carries

over from common usage connotations that are irrelevant and misleading in literary discourse. It is so easy to think of style in writing as we think of stylish clothes—something that can be purchased and carried home in a package, something that can be put on or taken off at will, a kind of rich, even bespangled robe with which any, even the most unprepossessing, body of thought can be hastily dressed up and made presentable. The word tends to fix the attention on what is superficial and decorative in writing, upon verbal felicity and the neat phrase; whereas in reality the foundation of good writing is organic structure—logical arrangement and continuity in the sentence, the paragraph, the chapter, the book as a whole. All this is a matter, not of happy phrasing alone or primarily, but of clear and logical thinking. Good form, in short, is a matter of mastering the content, of exploring with infinite patience every part of the subject, in all of its ramifications, letting the mind respond, with as much suppleness as may be, to the form and pressure of the matter in hand. The style, if there is to be any worth mentioning, must wait upon the idea, which is itself form as well as substance.

How common and how false is the notion that style and thought, form and substance, are distinct and separable aspects of literary discourse. The truth is, as Henry James says, that "form is substance to that degree that there is absolutely no substance without it." Of course we can often enough distinguish between the substance or thought which the author had in his mind and intended to convey in the form of words, and the substance or thought which he actually does convey in the words used. But that is another matter. Taking any writing as it

stands, apart from any inference or guess as to what the author intended to say, there is no thought or substance there except as it is given by the style or form of words used to express it. In this sense form and substance, style and thought are inseparable, and if you change the one, you change, to that extent, the other.

Take a trivial example. Ten or a dozen years ago I picked up and read, to pass the time, a popular novel— one of those novels pronounced, by critics who read nothing but the jacket blurbs, an important creative work of art. In six months it was forgotten, and I do not now remember even the title or the name of the author. But I do remember (and to that extent it was important for me) this sentence: "Bess was expecting her third child within the month, and she was feeling done up." Well, I should think she might be feeling done up. It is unusual for a woman to have, or to expect to have, three children within a month. You may say, oh well, we know what the author meant. Of course we do. We know perfectly well what the author meant. But we know it, not from what is found in the sentence as written, but as an inference from our general knowledge of women and childbirth. We know, that is to say, what the author *must* have meant. But taking the sentence as it stands, apart from this inference, there are two possible meanings; and we can therefore say that the style is bad because the thought is obscure, or that the thought is obscure because the style is bad. We can't make the thought clear without changing the style, or make the style good without clarifying the thought. We can make both thought and style good by this simple change: "Bess was expecting, within the month, her third child, and she was feeling done up."

How did we achieve this result? Did we first decide what good style is, and then apply it to the thought? I think not. I think we first decided precisely what the thought to be conveyed was, and then found a form of words that would convey it without ambiguity.

How, then, does one, as the saying is, cultivate a good style? Chiefly, I think, by not trying to cultivate it as something apart from the thought: chiefly, that is to say, by concentrating on thought or substance, on the assumption that, if the thought or substance is fully mastered, the style will take care of itself. Good style in writing is like happiness in living—something that comes to you, if it comes at all, only if you are preoccupied with something else: if you deliberately go after it you will probably not get it. What the writer should be chiefly preoccupied with is clear and exact thinking, and then with finding the form of words, without asking whether they conform to some standard of good style, which will convey fully and exactly the thought which he wishes to convey. If he can do that the style is bound to be good, as good, that is to say, as the quality of the thought permits. There is no one style that is good for all purposes. Metaphor has its uses, but it is out of place in describing a machine—or a battle, even if Shakespeare did use it for that purpose. The good style is the style that is suited for expressing whatever it is—matter of fact, idea, emotion—that in the particular instance needs to be expressed: "proper words in proper places."

Suppose, for example, that I am sitting, on a calm summer night, in a garden, looking at a bank of flowers flooded with moonlight. You ask me to describe what I see there. Well, perhaps I am a literal, unimaginative

fellow who sees nothing there except the literal, commonplace fact. So I say: "The moon is shining on the bank." Is that a good style? Given the thought to be expressed, it is a very good style. I might say: "On the bank the moon is shining"; but that is not the natural order in English. Or I might say: "Comes the moon shining on the bank." But that isn't true: the moon doesn't come, it remains where it is. No, for the thought to be expressed the style is as good as it can be. But then I may not be as literal and unimaginative as all that. Maybe I went to college and studied science. What I see there in the garden suggests to me an idea, and so I say: "The moonlight on the bank is a reflection of the sun's light." This style is as good as the other, but the form of words is different because the idea to be expressed is different.

But again, suppose I am another fellow altogether. I am Lorenzo, in love with Jessica, sitting with her in the garden, looking at the moonlight on the bank. For Lorenzo, under those circumstances, that is no ordinary bank and no ordinary moonlight. For Lorenzo there is some poignant beauty there which, if he could find the right words to express his feeling about it, would convey just what it means to him to be in love with Jessica and to be sitting with her there in the garden in the moonlight. Like any lover, he does the best he can, and, with the aid of Shakespeare, he finds the perfect form: "How sweet the moonlight sleeps upon that bank!" This is good style too, not because it is a succession of felicitous sounds, but because it expresses with perfection what lovers from time immemorial have felt, on calm summer nights, about moonlight and gardens when sitting in them with their Jessicas. It is good style for the same reason that the other

examples are good style: because it expresses exactly the idea that is there to be expressed. If it is better style than the others, it is so only because the idea is more subtle, or more interesting, or more universal in its appeal.

The point of all this, and the substance of all I have to say about good writing, is first to have something of your own to say, and then say it in your own way. But this advice is easier to give than to follow. The catch is in the words "your own." It is relatively easy to have something to say and to say it; but difficult to be sure that what you have to say is your own, or that you are saying it in your own way. The reason is that we are all, to borrow a stereotype from the sociologists, socially conditioned, which means, I suppose, that we are all under a certain pressure, from the social group or profession to which we belong, to think as the group thinks, and to use the clichés that the group understands: so that we easily become habituated to certain conventional patterns of thought and stereotyped forms of expressions. Any one who wishes to have something of his own to say and to say it in his own way must avoid, as a sin against the Holy Ghost, these conventional patterns of thought and stereotyped forms of expression.

Some of them are fairly easy to avoid because they are so obvious and so unlovely, and have so often been pointed out by the literary guild, as horrendous examples of how not to do it. There is the stilted, archaic legal style, with its *whereases* and *hereinbefore mentioneds,* its *said parties of the second part,* and *wherefore be it understoods.* There is the business style, so deadly and so efficiently dead. "Your esteemed favor of even date received, and beg to inform you. Dictated but not read."

To which the proper reply, I've always thought, would be: "Your esteemed favor of even date received. Opened, but not yet, and please God never will be, read."

And then, of course, there is the academic style dear to professors. Perhaps you have sometimes wondered how we get that way. Well, I will try to tell you, although it isn't easy. One thing is that people rather expect professors, more than other people, to tell the exact truth, and they rather expect them to be pretty solemn about it and use long words in the telling. This often puts us on the spot, because it sometimes isn't easy to tell the exact truth in long words, and if you tell the truth in simple words it often sounds very funny, and professors can't afford, as Henry Adams told me forty years ago, to get a reputation for being funny. Let me illustrate. For some months before I came to Northampton, many people were asking me what I was going to do at Smith College. To most of them I said I was going to Smith College to do a little teaching and historical research. Well, this was true, in a way, and it sounded perfectly all right. But it wasn't the unvarnished truth; and if you will promise not to give me away, I will give you the low-down: I came to Smith College to be well paid for having a good time. If a professor persists in telling the funny old truth in that simple way, he will soon find himself qualified to write a book on "How to Lose Friends and Irritate People." And so, in order not to disappoint people we get into the habit of wrapping up the truth in the academic style. What I should have said, of course, was that I had been honored with a call from Smith College to occupy the William Allan Neilson Research Professorship, which was founded for

the promotion of learning and teaching. That is true, as far as it goes; but it stops soon enough to leave the impression that the professor is what he is expected to be, a learned and serious fellow.

But there is more to it than that. The fact is that we are fairly learned fellows; and the academic style comes natural to us because we know so much. Knowing so much, we cannot easily think of any particular thing without thinking at the same time of everything it is related to in heaven and earth; and so the concrete instance, regarded in this broad way, is a nuisance until, divested of all that makes it vivid and alive, we can sub-subsume it in a generalized statement. Aware that there is much to be said on the one hand, and equally much to be said on the other, we feel the need of safeguarding even the simplest affirmation by triple qualifications, remote historical allusions, and parenthetical cross references. To say simply that a spade is a spade gives us the naked, exposed feeling of being out on a limb on a hot day. We therefore instinctively take refuge in the cold, spare chambers of the abstract, edging in by means of the indirect order, the passive verb, and the ablative absolute. Do not expect us to say that a spade is a spade. We know so much more than that about a spade; and it is not the desire to show off, but the desire to tell the complete and exact truth that leads us to give the spade all we have— "The hand tool in question, employed from time immemorial (as the best evidence permits us to suppose) for purposes of excavation, is in our own time, at least among English-speaking peoples, commonly referred to as a spade." Since we know so much about a spade, it is really rather cruel to expect us, in describing

it, to leave out everything except what is strictly relevant. With all of these stereotypes we are familiar, and on the present occasion we don't need to worry about them. We don't need to worry about them because, for the present occasion, we are neither lawyers nor business men nor professors, but literary fellows—the very literary fellows who have so often made merry over the unlovely style affected by these gentry. We will avoid all the stereotypes because we know them all.

But wait a minute, do we? Haven't we perhaps forgotten the literary stereotypes, the most dangerous of all for us because they are less obvious than the others and far more difficult to avoid: less obvious, because they are not in themselves unlovely; more difficult to avoid, because we have unconsciously filled our minds with them by reading the very best literature.

Let me make this concrete. Suppose I am a college student, and that the instructor in advanced English composition has assigned me the topic, "A Day in the Woods." But it happens that, coming fresh from the Iowa prairies, I have never seen a woods, much less spent a day in them. You think that should stop me from writing an essay about a day in the woods? Not at all. I have never spent a day in the woods, but I have spent many days in the alcove where the English classics are kept. Therefore I know plenty about the woods without ever having seen any. I know that the woods are filled with giant oaks and stately hickories and graceful elms, with aromatic spruces exuding medicinal gums, with birches whose smooth greenish-gray bark, coated with dank moss, has the texture of velvet. I know that in the woods are inviting paths, carpeted with dead leaves and

pine spills—paths that lead to the heart of the woods, far from the busy haunts of men, where perchance one many find a shady bower, beside a purling brook. I know that while men may come and men may go, the brook goes on forever, and that since it burbles it must be shallow, because still water runs deepest. I know that here, in the heart of the woods, eternal silence dwells, and that all nature is pervaded with a delightful woodsy odor.

Since I know all this, what more do I need for a day in the woods? Well, of course I need a maiden—a maiden fair and fancy free, with yellow hair hanging down her back like ripe corn. In Iowa corn never means wheat, but always Indian corn that does not resemble braided hair in the least. No matter. If her hair is yellow it has to be like ripe corn. However, it doesn't have to be yellow. It may be naturally wavy, rebellious to the wind, and black as a raven's wing. In any case, the maiden must have frank, but merry and sparkling eyes, cheeks like Baldwin apples, and a trim figure simply but attractively garbed in a gingham dress. Thoughtfully anticipating our needs, the maiden has prepared a basket, I mean a hamper, packed with simple but wholesome and appetizing viands. With a courtesy native to a son of the soil living close to Nature, I gallantly relieve the maiden of the hamper, and together we make our way over hill and dale to the forest, and tread the trackless paths to the heart of the woods, where, beside the babbling brook we spend the day in careless but innocent abandon; and only when the sun is declining in the west, and the tall trees begin to lay their shadows like arms along the ground, do we regretfully return, arriving

at our destination as the daylight fades into dusk, physically fatigued, but spiritually refreshed and happy from our day in the woods.

The essay, you must admit, is a good one, and merits grade "A" for literary excellence. It is a good essay because it was easy to write, and it was easy to write because I had never spent a day in the woods. It would have been far more difficult to write if I had actually spent a day in the woods with the dame. Native curiosity might have betrayed me into looking at the woods. I might have noticed that the trees were too close together to permit the oaks to become giants or the elms graceful. The spruces might have exuded, instead of medicinal gums, a hornet's nest. The delightful woodsy smell, had I stopped to analyze it, might have proved to be compounded of mould, rotting lumber, and dead skunk. We might have found plenty of underbrush but not paths. The shady bower in the heart of the woods might have been no more than the least unpleasant place to sit down; and the purling brook might have had all the appearance of a stagnant pond covered with slime and filling the air with mosquitoes. If, as might well have happened, it began to rain at two o'clock, we should have returned earlier than we had intended but by no means regretfully, and in any case wet and bedraggled. Probably the dame would have had runs in her stockings, and maybe a bee sting on her nose. We would have arrived at our destination, I should think, pretty low in our minds, and fed up with each other, and would have parted with a sigh of relief, and a mutual "that's that, and it's a washout."

The point is that the essay would have been a washout

too. Having found out that the New Forest is not the same thing as the woods in Wisconsin, the ideas of Tennyson and Shakespeare about the woods would have been sadly disarranged in my mind. I should have had to sort out my impressions of the day actually spent in the woods, and find words of my own to express them: and what I had to say about the day actually spent in the woods would almost certainly not have been fit to hand in to the instructor in advanced English composition. It is possible even that I should not have been able to write the essay at all, since my chief difficulty would have been the same as that which confronted Orlando, whose story Virginia Woolf has related. Orlando was writing, and soon, says Virginia Woolf, "he had convered ten pages with poetry. He was fluent, evidently, but he was abstract. There was never a word said as he himself would have said it, but all was turned with a fluency and sweetness which, considering his age . . . was remarkable enough. At last, however, he came to a halt. He was describing, as all young poets are forever describing, nature, and in order to match the shade of green precisely he looked (and here he showed more audacity than most) at the thing itself, which happened to be a laurel bush growing beneath the window. After that, of course, he could write no more. Green in nature is one thing, in literature another."

The moral is that readers and writers of books live in an atmosphere filled with lurking literary chichés. Avoid them if possible. Remember that you have never seen an Elizabethan cat, and that modern cats are not always necessary, or necessarily harmless. The moral is that if you wish to say something of your own about

a cat, or about nature, take a look at it. Take a long
look. Flaubert told De Maupassant that before trying to
decribe a tree he should look at it until he could see
it as no one else had ever seen it. His description would
then have merit because it would have character. Something of the author would be in it; both thought and style
would be, to that extent, the man himself. How much
of our writing is good—clear, logical, forceful, even
felicitous and witty—but lacking this one thing—character. Its excellence is a conventional, that is to say, a
borrowed excellence. Neither the thought nor the style
is, strictly speaking, the author's own, but a kind of
ersatz, a synthetic product of the best that has been
thought and said about the subject.

The moral is, be yourself. When covering ten pages,
forget about the original ideas that Ernest Hemingway
or Professor Einstein might be expected to have on the
subject, and the excellent style they might use to express
their ideas. Try to understand clearly what you yourself,
Jane Smith, know or think or feel about the subject,
and then express it in a form of words that is natural to
you, a form of words that your friends might conceivably
recognize as the authentic style of Jane Smith. If you
can do that, the style will be as good as it can be, because
it will be as good as Jane Smith is. Of course, Jane Smith
may not be very good; but be sure of this: that by no
effort to write as some one else writes, by no borrowed
mannerisms, or current tricks of the trade, can the
writing of Jane Smith ever be essentially better than
she is. But be sure of this also: if she takes life as it
comes, on the chin, if she works hard, reads and observes
with attention, thinks honestly, if she becomes absorbed

in something more important than she is—if she does all this, Jane Smith will have to be very bad indeed if she does not become, perhaps not every day in every way, but at least every year in some way, better and better. And as Jane Smith becomes better, her style (good-bye and good riddance to the word) will get better too.

Letters on Education

1. CARL BECKER TO JAMES W. GLEED

In October 1916 the Visiting Committee to the Alumni Association of the University of Kansas, in connection with its regular activities, invited Carl Becker and several other former University of Kansas Professors to comment on conditions within the University. Carl Becker had left Kansas at the end of the school year in 1916, and when he made his reply he was teaching at the University of Minnesota. In a covering note to his lengthy comments, Becker stated: "I have spoken freely, and I need not say that when I am outside of Kansas I do not give expression to these views, but make out the best case I can for the state and the university for which I have a real regard."

November 20, 1916 *

DEAR MR. GLEED,

In reply to your letter of inquiry, I wish to say first of all that personally I have no grievance of any kind against the university or any one connected with it. I

---

* This letter is a part of the James W. Gleed Manuscripts at the University of Kansas; it is printed here by permission of the Library of the University of Kansas and the Cornell University Library.

came to the university fourteen years ago, as Assistant Professor, at a salary of $800. During those years, the recognition I received, in the way a promotion and raise of salary, and in every way, was all that I could hope for and more than I could reasonably expect. My relations with the students, the faculty, and the university administrative officers, have been of the most friendly and cordial character. I liked the people of Kansas, and have many good friends in the state, and particularly in Lawrence where I had come to feel, as you can well imagine, very much at home. Under the circumstances, therefore, it is hardly necessary to say that I left the university with great regret, after mature deliberation, and on account of conditions which seemed to me most deplorable and not likely to be corrected in the near future.

I take it that a good university is primarily a question of getting first-rate scholars and teachers for its faculty. Of course you have to have buildings and equipment, but you may have the finest material plant and still have a very poor university; whereas, if you have a faculty of able scholars and teachers you will have a good university even with very inferior buildings and equipment. When I came to Kansas there were then, or had recently been, connected with the university a number of men who gave distinction to the institution. I recall Chancellor Snow, Professors Williston, Franklin, Kellogg, McClung, Caruth, Marvin, Barber, Hodder, Templin, and A. T. Walker; there may have been others whom I do not now think of. Hodder, Templin, and Walker are still there. The others are no longer there, and it is not too much to say that they have not been replaced by men of equal, or nearly equal distinction. There are

many good men on the faculty, it is true, but it would be impossible now to duplicate the above list, whereas, since the faculty is so much larger now than it was then, it should be possible to double it. For fourteen years there has been much talk of the marvellous growth of the university, meaning always growth in numbers, forgetting that quality is the essential thing. Taking the institution as a whole, considering it from the point of view of the quality of its faculty, and this means the quality of the work done, both in teaching and in productive scholarship, the university is not, in my opinion, as good an institution as it was fourteen years ago.

What is the cause of this deterioration? Some would say lack of money. I do not think so. No university has all the money it needs, and Kansas has been no exception to this rule. But during fourteen years the appropriations have steadily increased; and it is a well known fact that for many years Chancellor Strong got precisely what he asked for, which was what he regarded as essential. With these funds in hand, it was possible to do one of two things; either to apply them to maintaining and strengthening the departments already established, or to apply them, or a considerable part of them, to establishing new departments. The latter policy is the one that has been more or less consistently followed. Now, inasmuch as the number of students has increased as steadily as the appropriations, new departments could not be taken on without neglecting the legitimate needs of those already existing. It seems to me obvious, therefore, that the Medical School, the Extension Department, the Department of Journalism, and the School of Education were established at the expense of the legitimate

needs of the college, the Graduate School, the Law School, and the School of Engineering.

It would have been bad policy, under the circumstances, to undertake this expansion even if there had been some real need for it. I cannot think there was any real need for it. A good medical school is a good thing; but a poor one is worse than none. A medical school is immensely expensive; no other sort of education is anything like as expensive; and yet there never was, and never was much prospect of there being, a tithe of the money necessary for a good four-year medical course at Kansas. Even now it is a fair question whether it would not be wise policy to abandon the most expensive part of the school, the last two years, and concentrate upon the first two years. There was, in my opinion, even less need of an extension department. Evidently the legislature thinks so too; for, so I was credibly informed, it has refused, during the last two bienniums, to pass the special appropriation asked for this department. For certain kinds of extension work, there is a real demand; but this work was done, and still is done I am told, by the particular departments concerned. It would seem, therefore, that the only reason for organizing a special department of extension was to push out upon the state a kind of activities for which there was no real demand, scarcely any demand at all except a fictitious demand manufactured largely at the university. What is the need of a special department of journalism? Young men are there taught, for the most part, precisely what they would have to learn, and would easily learn, in a newspaper office—the mechanics of printing, the knack of getting news, and of warping facts to make a

good story. They ought to get in the university the things they can't get in a newspaper office, the things they never will get adequately if they do not get them in a university. What they need, if they wish to be anything more than smart reporters, is a fundamental grounding in history, economics, English literature, politics and law. A very good course for prospective journalists could be made on the basis of these subjects; but a department of journalism, by stressing the superficial things, makes it less possible for the student to get as much of these subjects as he should. What does the School of Education do that was not done by the Department of Education which we formerly had? Formerly one professor and perhaps two assistants offered the courses necessary to enable prospective teachers to get the 12 hours of education required for the teacher's diploma. Now four professors and three assistants offer the courses enabling prospective teachers to get the 15 hours of required education. As far as I can see, the chief result of establishing a school of education was to make seven men grow where only three grew before. Last spring I sat on a committee of which the chairman was the Dean of the School of Education; and he made a strong plea for lowering the requirements for the degree in Education on the ground that otherwise the professors could not get students enough to keep them busy. He did not put it in those words, but that is what his proposal came to.

What pressure Chancellor Strong was under, from the alumni, the regents, or the legislature, to adopt a policy of expansion, I do not know; but it seems to me that it would have been much wiser to have devoted the resources of the university to the departments already

existing, and to two things particularly, to procuring the very ablest scholars to be had, and to building up a library adequate to their needs. A first-rate mathematician, Professor Young, came to Kansas for a year; he went to Dartmouth with little if any increase in salary. One of the ablest men Kansas ever had was M. A. Barber, a man whose scientific work is better known in Germany than it is in Kansas. I knew him well, and I think he would have remained if there had been any proper attitude towards scientific research. A few years ago Dick Scammon was at Kansas; they let him go for a trifling salary, and he is now full Professor here in Minnesota, and is regarded as one of the ablest men in the university. They tried to get rid of W. U. Moore; he now draws a salary of [$]6000 in the Columbia Law School. Professor Kay, a man of force, and highly regarded by geologists throughout the country, was allowed to go to Iowa. These men should have been kept; they would have been of more value to Kansas than a wilderness of extension departments and schools of education. And most of them could have been kept had there been a proper attitude towards productive scholarship and a proper effort to encourage it.

But if you wish to get good men and to encourage scholarship and research, the library is of primary importance. A good library, and plenty of money for books, are as attractive as high salary to the genuine scholar. What is the situation of Kansas in respect to the library? There is scarcely a weaker spot in the university. Amherst College, with a student body of about 500, has a better library than Kansas. For fourteen years it has been impossible to get anything done about it, that is

to say, about the very thing that cannot be neglected without serious prejudice to any university. Money for books is a crying need at Kansas, and second to that a competent librarian. Last year the budget carried $3,000 which we were told could be used for a librarian. A first-rate man could almost certainly have been had, Mr. Koch, formerly of Michigan. Millis and Hodder and some others did their level best to have him offered the position. But nothing was done. At least $50,000 a year for books would not be too much, it would not be enough, but it would do much to remedy a situation that is the despair of every scholar on the faculty. If this seems a big sum, it must be remembered that all new state universities are at a tremendous disadvantage compared with such schools as Harvard and Yale. Those institutions got the great sets and collections long ago when they were much easier to be had than now, and they profit constantly by munificent private donations. If Kansas would concentrate on men, books, and scientific equipment, she would soon gather there, to reinforce the real scholars which she now has, a group of men who would initiate the activities and create the atmosphere that go to make a real university.

What chance is there of this being done under the present management? None whatever. On the contrary, the present management has accentuated, and will continue to accentuate, the very evils which I have mentioned. A paid board, I say a *paid* board and not a single board, is a great mistake. The reason is simple. First, you cannot get the ablest men in Kansas to abandon their professions to give all their time to this business. Second, those who do take the positions, giving all their

time and receiving a high salary, are almost bound to feel that it is necessary to justify their highly paid position. They feel that they must earn their salaries. And they know no other way to do it except by taking an active and responsible part in the management of the university, in directing its policy, in employing its faculty, in applying its funds.

Now, these men, in spite of the best intentions which are admitted, are not competent to take the initiative. I don't suppose Mr. Hackney would think himself competent to take over the management of a highly specialized and intricate business industry, of which he had only such a general knowledge as any good lawyer might be supposed to have. But a university is a far more difficult, as well as a far more important matter than, let us say, a meat-packing industry. Men who have all their lives been intimately associated with universities, who have given all their intelligence and energy to the problem of education, find that problem an extremely complex and difficult one. How is it possible that Mr. Hackney (and this is nothing to the disparagement of Mr. Hackney), how is it possible that Mr. Hackney, who wouldn't think himself competent to run a meat-packing industry, should be thought competent to run a university? A board of Regents such as we formerly had, under no obligation to justify their job, under no obligation to anybody, composed of men to whom the state was rather under obligation for giving their time for nothing, such men, working in harmony with the Chancellor and the faculty, leaving them the initiative but giving them the benefit, and the very great benefit, of the practical layman's point of view, were of the

highest assistance. But a paid board, setting the Chancellor aside, leaving him without power and without responsibility, is bound to do things on its own hook, and so far as it does is bound to make a mess of it.

The present board deserves credit for what it has not done. It has not done many things on its own hook. But it has virtually set the Chancellor aside, with this result: in so far as the Board doesn't take a hand the university simply drifts; in so far as it does take a hand the result is deplorable for the most part. The Board has made a number of high appointments in the university contrary to the Chancellor's advice; these appointments have been, to put it mildly, very unfortunate, with one possible exception. I never saw any evidence that the Board ever took any intelligent interest in, or was really aware of the existence of, the genuinely valuable work done at the university; but they have almost invariably exhibited, in their enthusiasms and in their official decisions, a marked partiality for the superficial aspects of educational activities. I was told that an official report of the Board, published last fall, found its way into the faculty club at the University of Chicago, and was read there to his colleagues by one of the members, to an accompaniment of derisive laughter. I can well believe the story. There is not a line in the report which indicates that the author had the faintest conception of what a university should be, or that he had any knowledge of the real scholarly work that is being done in the University of Kansas. It was apparently designed to show that everything was now quite as it should be, and that this happy result was due largely to the changes effected by the Board of Administration.

This is the way the situation looks to me; and so far as I can judge it is much the way it looks to the good men on the faculty. I am forty-three years old. The next ten or fifteen years are important ones for me. Why should I, having a fair opportunity to go elsewhere, have remained in an institution so largely at the mercy of the incompetent, an institution without wise and farsighted leadership, an institution where the genuine is so largely ignored while the sham and the shoddy are exhalted. The University of Minnesota is by no means one of the best universities in the country. In many ways it suffers from the same weaknesses as Kansas. But it is largely directed by the President and the Faculty. In the last six years it has been going forward instead of backward; and the prospects here for the next ten years are, so far as one can judge, very good. I have many good friends throughout the country, east and west, whose advice I asked; every one of them, without hesitation, gave it as his opinion that it would be wise for me to make the change.

It may be that I have misjudged the situation. It may be that Kansas will get rid of her paid board, and that during the next ten years she will forge ahead and attain the position among the universities of the country which the intelligence of the people of Kansas and the traditions they have inherited lead one to think she ought to occupy. If this should come about, no one would be more pleased than I would be.

Very sincerely,
CARL BECKER

2. CARL BECKER TO THE *CORNELL DAILY SUN*

In the Cornell Daily Sun *of December 6, 1926, "Five Un-happy and Bewildered Freshmen" complained that the Christmas holidays were approaching and they had no more idea what their college education was all about than when they first entered Cornell University. The editors of the* Sun *used the bewildered freshmen as a take-off for two long editorials (December 6 and 8) advocating an orientation course in the Arts College. Carl Becker responded to the bewildered freshmen and the proposed orientation course with a letter (December 10) on the inevitability of uncertainty in modern education.*

To the Editor of the *Cornell Daily Sun:*

I was interested in the letter of Five Bewildered Freshmen and in the discussion it gave rise to. The freshmen say they have been engaged in the intellectual life for more than two months and don't know what it's all about. This is bad, but who is to blame? Some say the students are to blame, and some say the professors. What is to be done about it? You suggest . . . an orientation course such as is given in other universities.

For my part, I don't blame anyone—not the freshmen, certainly. It's not especially the student's fault if he doesn't know what it's all about. If he did, he wouldn't need to come to college. That's why, I have always supposed, young people come to college—to get some notion, even if only a glimmering, of what it's about. They come to get "oriented." But why expect to be oriented in two months, or a year? The whole four

years' college course is a course in orientation. It isn't a very satisfactory one, indeed. Four years isn't enough. Life itself is scarcely long enough to enable one to find out what it's all about.

Neither do I blame the professors—not particularly. Many people appear to think that professors possess some secret of knowledge and wisdom which would set the students right as to the meaning of things if they would only impart it. This, I do assure you, is an illusion. I could write you a letter on behalf of Five Bewildered Professors which would make the five bewildered freshmen appear cocksure by comparison. The professors are in the same boat. They don't know either what it's all about. They tried to find out when in college, and they have been trying ever since. Most of them, if they are wise, don't expect ever to find out, not really. But still they will, if they are wise, keep on trying. That is, indeed, just what the intellectual life is—a continuous adventure of the mind in which something is being discovered possessing whatever meaning the adventurer can find in it.

This effort to find out what it's all about is, in our time, more difficult than ever before. The reason is that the old foundations of assured faith and familiar custom are crumbling under our feet. For four hundred years the world of education and knowledge rested securely on two fundamentals which were rarely questioned. These were *Christian philosophy* and *Classical learning*. For the better part of a century Christian faith has been going by the board, the Classical learning into the discard. To replace these we have as yet no foundations, no certainties. We live in a world of incredibly rapid change, a world of naturalistic science and of physico-chemico-libido psy-

chology. There are no longer any certainties either in life or in thought. Everywhere confusion. Everywhere questions. Where are we? Where did we come from? Where do we go from here? What is it all about? The freshmen are asking, and they may well ask. Everyone is asking. No one knows; and those who profess with most confidence to know are most likely to be mistaken. Professors could reorganize the College of Arts if they knew what a College of Arts should be. They could give students a "general education" if they knew what a general education was, or would be good for if one had it. Professors are not especially to blame because the world has lost all certainty about these things.

One of the sure signs that the intellectual world is bewildering is that everywhere, in colleges and out, people are asking for "Orientation" courses which will tell the freshmen straight off what it is all about. If we were oriented we shouldn't need such courses. This does not mean that I am opposed to an orientation course for freshmen. I would like an orientation course for freshmen. I would like one for seniors. I would like one for professors and trustees. I would like one for President Farrand and President Butler. Only, who is to give it? And what is it to consist of? I asked Professor Hayes, "What about your orientation course at Columbia?" He said, "It's a good thing for the instructors who give it." I asked a man whose son had taken the course, "What did he get out of it?" The reply was, "He read three books in three unrelated fields of knowledge and got a kick out of one of them." Who knows the "background" or the "general field of knowledge?" If the course is given by many professors the student will be taking several courses

as one course instead of several courses as separate courses. If one man gives it what will it be? It will be as good as the man is. If we could get a really top-notch man to give a course, no matter what, and call it an orientation course, I should welcome it. H. G. Wells might give such a course, and it would be a good course. I doubt if it would orient anyone or settle anything, but it would stir the students up and make them think. That would be its great merit. That is the chief merit of any course— that it unsettles students, makes them ask questions.

The Five Bewildered Freshmen have got more out of their course than they know. It has made them ask a question— What is it all about? That is a pertinent question. I have been asking it for thirty-five years, and I am still as bewildered as they are.

CARL BECKER

In the Sun *of December 13, 1926, Marshall M. Knappen, then a Cornell graduate student in history and at the time in the Congregational ministry, took exception to Becker's view that the Christian faith no longer provided modern life with certainty, that uncertainty was inescapable in modern life and education. Becker responded (December 15) to Mr. Knappen's letter by amplifying and clarifying his position on education. At the same time time, however, he politely withdrew from any possible debate on the relevance of the Christian faith as an explanation of modern life.*

To THE EDITOR OF THE *Cornell Daily Sun:*

May I take a little space to say that Mr. Knappen has apparently misunderstood me in two important respects. First, as to "certainties in life and thought," and Christian philosophy "going by the board." Of course there are certainties in life and thought for the individual. I have

many of my own, although Mr. Knappen appears to think not. Of course there are many people who have an assured Christian faith and an assured Christian philosophy. But which of these so many and conflicting certainties in life and thought, which of these so many and diverse versions of Christian faith shall the college teach? Formerly the educated and learned world was fairly well agreed as to what a college should teach in order to give the student a "general education." It should teach Latin, Greek, Mathematics, and the Evidences of Christianity. Is it not evident that there is no longer any agreement, either in college or outside of it, that these are the essentials of a college course? My point is only that Christian philosophy and Classical learning are "going by the board" as the commonly accepted foundations of a "general education." This seems to me merely the statement of obvious fact. Personally, I am strong for the teaching of Latin and Greek, and mathematics; and I think that a philosophy of life, whether Christian or other, is what a student should mainly seek in his college course.

The second point. Mr. Knappen appears to think that I wish students to accept my "findings"—my ideas, my point of view, my philosophy of life. Heaven forbid! The main point of my letter was that college offers the student an opportunity (not so good an opportunity as we all wish) to enlarge his experience, extend his knowledge, to be initiated into many points of view, many philosophies of life. I would not have the student tamely accept any professor's "findings." He cannot accept all that are offered since there are so many and conflicting ones offered. The student must, with whatever aid he can get from professors, work out his own philosophy. The col-

lege does not offer all these various and conflicting points of view in order to confuse the student. It offers them because they exist in modern thought, and the college necessarily reflects the conditions of modern thought. In any case, a philosophy which the student accepts on authority, whether the authority of a professor or of a faculty, is not in my opinion worth much. The student who manages to work out any sort of philosophy of life during his four years has got the most a modern college can give him. Mr. Knappen has obviously done just that. It is what I wish every student to do.

CARL BECKER

3. CARL BECKER TO *TIME* MAGAZINE

Time magazine used to publish the letters it received separate from the magazine itself. In 1934 one Time *reader wrote an appreciative letter on Carl Becker, stating that he was an outstanding prose writer and that Becker's high school history book was used "as a reference work in graduate reading rooms."* Time *published the letter, adding to it a picture it mistakenly thought to be Becker and an editorial note. The note explained that Becker was a shy, retiring, but popular teacher at Cornell University who still "trembles" when he faces a class and who lectures "in a voice too weak to fill the room." Becker, the editor reported, seldom reveals his own opinion on history. "During a course in European History from 1815 to 1914 he made two comments—1) he referred to Theodore Roosevelt as 'my hero'; 2) he admired Bismarck's honesty in admitting how unscrupulously he had altered the Ems telegram." The editor went on to say that Becker opposed "such academic restrictions on liberty as roll calls, examinations, required papers"; "he has been known*

to forget to give examinations, requires no work at all in his seminars, but gets it nonetheless." To all of this Becker responded with a letter Time *published in its* Letters *September 17, 1934.*

SIRS:

Thanks for sending me a copy of *Letters*, Aug. 20, in which you published some remarks about me and a picture with my name under it. As Huck Finn said about the book "wrote" by Tom Sawyer, this account tells the truth "mainly," but nevertheless contains some "whoppers." Graduate students may read my *Modern History,* but I feel sure no professor of history would so far forget the decencies as to use a high-school textbook "as a reference work in graduate reading rooms." Thirty years ago it was an ordeal for me to face a class, but it no longer is so. I do not "tremble." On the contrary, nothing is more restful for me or, I should imagine, for the students either, than my lectures in modern history which are given at 3 P.M., a proper hour I have always thought for the siesta. If I cannot be heard beyond the front rows, so much the better, since no one wishes to be disturbed when taking a nap.

I am not opposed to examinations. Examinations are very useful as a means of determining whether a student should have a degree, and a degree is a useful thing to have, although it has little or nothing to do with education. I get a reputation for being opposed to examinations because I insist on attributing to them the value which they have and not the value which they haven't. In any case I am sure I never forgot a scheduled undergraduate examination, although one of my assistants who was charged with holding one once did. I feel very strongly

about this, since faithfulness in small obligations is one of the minor virtues I cultivate assiduously in order to compensate for major defects.

Whoever said I referred to Theodore Roosevelt as "my hero" must be mistaken. No man is a hero to the scientific historian who valets him; and in any case if I had a hero it would certainly not be a verbose purveyor of platitudes. By the way, the picture under which you have placed my name is not a picture of me at all. I suspect you got this from a group photograph, taken by a newspaper man, of those who were given honorary degrees at Yale University in 1932. I was in the second row from the front, I think, and the names attributed to all the persons in that row were wrong, owing to the circumstances that the man who took the picture was given the names in the wrong order, which in turn was owing to the circumstance that two Yale professors, for what reason I don't know, were standing in that row as if they too were receiving honorary degrees on that day, which they were not. . . .

All of this reminds me of a story.

One morning a newspaper man remarked to his landlady: "The buckwheat cakes this year are not very good. It's not your fault. The buckwheat is not so good this year on account of the dry weather in August." "Oh, no," the landlady replied. "The buckwheat this year is just like always." The newspaper man then went down to the office and wrote for his paper an article on the current year's buckwheat crop, explaining that it was of inferior quality because of the dry weather in August. Upon returning home in the evening his landlady remarked brightly. "You was right about the buckwheat. I

just now read in the paper where it said the buckwheat was spoiled on account of the dry spell in August."

Ten or 20 years hence graduate students will probably still be engaged in "scientific historical research," writing doctor's theses in which every statement of fact is supported by "the testimony of two independent witnesses not self-deceived." Such testimony will no doubt be found, then as now, in the "original sources," and no doubt newspapers will, then as now, be included among the original sources. This is nothing against the newspapers. As a historian I know how difficult it is to find out the truth about anything, and considering the conditions under which newspaper men have to work the wonder is that they get things as straight as they do.

CARL BECKER

III

ON DEMOCRACY

Why De Tocqueville
Wrote *Democracy in*
America

IN 1830, at the age of twenty-five, Alexis de Tocqueville was appointed to the not unimportant position of assistant *juge auditeur* of the tribunal of Versailles. The next year he obtained permission to visit the United States, ostensibly to inspect its prisons, in fact to observe at first hand its social and political institutions. The result of this visit was the publication (1835–1840) of *De la démocratie en Amérique*, the most famous, and perhaps the most penetrating, commentary on the United States ever made by a European observer. Why did this young French aristocrat leave the straight path leading to an established and honorable career in order to write a book about democracy in America? *

Being an honest man, Tocqueville does his best, in the

* This hitherto unpublished essay is printed by permission of the Cornell University Library.

Introduction to his book, to tell us why. Comparing his observations in the new world and the old, he says:

I saw [in Europe] an equality of conditions which, without having as in the United States reached its extreme limits, day by day became more extreme; and the same democratic government which dominated society in America appeared to me to be rapidly acquiring power in Europe.

From that moment I conceived the idea of the book which is now offered to the public. . . .

I have not even attempted to judge whether the social revolution . . . is beneficial or harmful to mankind; I have accepted this revolution as an accomplished fact, or on the point of being accomplished, and, among all the countries which have experienced it, I looked for the one in which its development has been most complete and peaceable, in order to discern clearly what its natural consequences are, and to discover, if possible, the means by which it may be made useful to men. I confess that in America I saw more than America; I sought there the image of democracy itself, of its tendencies, its character, its prejudices, its passions; I wished to understand it, if only to know what we have to hope for or to fear from it.[1]

Such is Tocqueville's own account of his reasons for writing *Democracy in America*. The account is true enough, yet it contrives to leave a somewhat false impression. He says that he did not even attempt to "judge whether the social revolution was beneficial or harmful to mankind"; but it would be a great mistake to suppose that Tocqueville was sufficiently objective not to *care* whether democracy was beneficial or harmful, to suppose that he was primarily interested in the social revolu-

[1] *Oeuvres complètes*, I, 2, 20.

tion as a phenomenon to be intellectually apprehended. Tocqueville was as honest, as "objective," as intent upon discovering the "truth," as any historian or social philosopher is likely to be; but the fact is that the question which he professed not to answer, the question whether democracy was beneficial or harmful to mankind, was precisely the question which occupied and distressed him more than any other. If he had never asked this question, or if, having asked it, he could have answered it offhand, as many men did, it would never have occurred to him to visit America or to write a book about it. The point is that Tocqueville found two conflicting answers to this question, and all his thinking about democracy was shaped by the compelling need to reconcile these conflicting answers, to find a "higher synthesis" which might include these "identical opposites." To understand why he wrote *Democracy in America,* to understand the "image of democracy itself" which he sought in the United States, we must know what these two conflicting answers were, and how Tocqueville tried to reconcile them.

One of the answers was given in immediate experience. Observed at close quarters, as it functioned in France and Europe about 1830, the social revolution seemed clearly a disintegrating force, something that was obviously levelling all the distinctions to which Tocqueville was attached, impairing all the values which he cherished. In despair he asked himself whether the world had always been what it was in his day—"a world in which there are no longer any fixed relations; a world in which virtue is unrelated to talent and talent unrelated to honor; a world in which love of order is confused with

the ambition of tyrants, and the love of liberty with contempt for law; a world in which conscience provides no more than an uncertain light for conduct; a world in which nothing any longer seems either prohibited, or permitted, or honest, or shameful, or true, or false." [2] No doubt conditions were somewhat better in the United States, a new country in which equality of material goods was relatively great, and could be accepted as a matter of course because distinctions of rank and birth had always been relatively unimportant. Nevertheless, even in the United States, where conditions are most favorable, what Tocqueville saw did not convince him that "government by the multitude is a good thing." [3]

This was one answer: judged by its results as disclosed to an intelligent observer, democracy was an evil thing. But unfortunately for his own peace of mind Tocqueville was a philosopher who believed in God; and it was therefore necessary for him to accommodate what appeared, in the temporal view, to be evil with what must, in its eternal aspects, be good. Like many men of his generation, Tocqueville was convinced that God's purposes were revealed, not merely in holy writ, but also in Nature, and not in Nature abstractly considered as the *philosophes* thought, but in Nature as exhibited in the experience of mankind. Immediate experience needed therefore to be supplemented and corrected by the study of history. Seen in a long-time perspective, the social revolution appeared to be no temporary diversion, prepared by the *philosophes* and imposed on an unsuspecting world by the crimes of the Jacobins, but an inevitable result of historical development. Seven centuries of

[2] *Op. cit.,* I, 18.   [3] *Op. cit.,* V, 316.

French history, and all of the kings (the able ones by their talents, the weak ones by their vices), had contributed to bring about, either with or in despite of the conscious purposes of men, this one result—"equality of conditions." This trend towards democracy, "the most persistent and continuous in all history," had thus all the characteristics of a preordained event. Who could then doubt that the social revolution was in accord with God's will? And if in accord with God's will then obviously designed for the benefit of mankind. Tocqueville therefore accepted democracy, by an act of faith, as somehow good, since he could more easily doubt the evidence of his own eyes than he could doubt of God's wisdom.[4]

Here then we have the two conflicting answers: judged by the evidence of his own eyes, Tocqueville found democracy evil; judged by the evidence of history, he found it somehow good. His distress was great because he could not easily doubt the evidence of his own eyes, and because he was unable to doubt the wisdom of God— unwilling, that is, to live in a world that appeared to be inevitably changing for the worse. He therefore tried desperately to dispose of this dilemma—to find good reasons for justifying democracy in spite of the fact that, so far as he could see, it never on its own initiative did anything to justify itself.

Tocqueville's solution of this problem was by no means original: it was, indeed, the solution commonly accepted by those nineteenth century Liberals who could not decide which they disliked most, the despotism of the one or the despotism of the many. It took the form of assuming that good and wise men might assist God a

---

[4] *Op. cit.,* I, 19.

little in carrying out his purposes. "In a word, it seems to me that democracy is henceforth a fact which a government may pretend to regulate, but not to arrest." [5] Since the inevitable trend of history must after all be implemented through the activities of men, it would be open to the better sort to manipulate events in such a way as to preserve what was best in a world that was obviously changing, but which, it was equally obvious, was in danger of changing too rapidly. Accept democracy, yes, in the sense that it was useless to try to put the clock back, to yearn with the Bonalds and the De Maistres for a return to the *ancien régime;* but to accept it with hands folded, that surely would be, for the intelligent, to renounce all social obligations. Supposing then that the trend towards equality of conditions had been decreed as a humane concession to common men, there could be no impiety in supposing that it might be guided, in some sense controlled, by the better sort in the interest of all concerned. In emancipating common men from servitude, God could not have intended to enslave the *élite;* in abrogating the despotism of a Louis XIV, he could not have intended to permit the more intolerable despotism of the mob. In short, if equality was within the divine plan somehow good, there must somehow be within the divine plan a place for liberty also.

To the preservation of liberty in a world committed to equality of conditions, Tocqueville therefore gave himself with passionate intensity. Liberty was for him, as for Lord Acton, a sacred word. "In speaking of liberty," says Sainte-Beuve, "his hand trembled, his voice vibrated with all the emotion of his being." [6] What, precisely, did

[5] *Op. cit.,* V, 316.   [6] *Causeries de lundi,* XV, 121.

Tocqueville mean by liberty? He never tells us really. The word symbolized values too profoundly felt to be objectively analyzed. But it is clear that he did not, like the protagonists of the Revolution, regard liberty and equality as two sides of the same shield, two interlocking principles equally essential to the realization of democracy. It is significant that Tocqueville commonly identified democracy with equality of conditions, the levelling of all superiorities, the obscuring of all distinctions; and in all that he says about the democratic revolution there is the implication that liberty is endangered by it. Tocqueville was after all an aristocrat; and however thoroughly convinced that the Revolution was an accomplished fact, he was well aware that, as Talleyrand said, no one who had not lived before 1789 could know how pleasant life could really be—for aristocrats. Like his eighteenth century forebears he therefore identified liberty with those distinctions which common men were apt to regard as special privileges, with those prerogatives which guaranteed for the leisured a way of life that was, or might be, spacious, urbane, and disinterested. Tocqueville's intelligence told him that the old order was done for, but his emotions persuaded him that the ideal values which were its only justification might still be safeguarded. Life seemed to him not worth living unless the inevitable trend of history towards equality of conditions could be accommodated to an "indeterminancy principle"—a little free play for the activities and values of a natural aristocracy, a cloistered place where honor and dignity and the disinterested pursuit of the impractical good might still be preserved from the contaminating touch of the vulgar.

This desired result would not come about of itself. How then were superior men to bring it about? By what concrete program could good and wise men preserve a measure of liberty in a world committed to equality of conditions? Tocqueville's answer to this question was simple in the extreme. He would mitigate the evils of democracy by a political device—the decentralization of governmental authority!

Instead of drifting day by day, content with the communal institutions provided by Napoleon, they [those in authority] should proceed at once to modify them, to turn over to the people gradually the management of their affairs . . . ; to *create local institutions* and above all to establish, if possible, those legal customs and ideas which are, in my opinion, the only bulwark against democracy.[7]

If this bulwark strikes us as singularly weak, we must remember that Tocqueville lived in an age when men had a singularly strong, if singularly naïve, faith in "constitutions," in the efficacy of political devices for the solution of social problems. It was an age in which Frenchmen more especially had an exaggerated respect for that species of local communal government which, supposed to be derived from the ancient Germanic Mark, was still preserved in the institutions of Anglo-Saxon countries, more particularly in England and the United States. For Tocqueville's purpose English experience was less relevant, since democracy was not completely established in England. It was in the United States that he could best observe the virtues of local government in a democratic society. This was no doubt why he saw

[7] *Oeuvres complètes*, V, 316.

in America "the very image of democracy itself"—that is to say, democracy as he wished to see it; for in America he could see a society in which equality was most fully established, and at the same time most competently checked and balanced by political devices, of which the most obvious was the decentralization of governmental authority.

It was thus not solely, or chiefly, to satisfy a scientific curiosity that Tocqueville went to America. "I wished to find there," he says in the Introduction to his book, "information from which we might profit." Naturally he found what he was looking for. The thing he found, the information from which France might profit, he tells us most explicitly in a private letter, written in 1836, to Louis de Kergorlay.

The ideas which you express [in opposition to centralized government] are the most vital of all my ideas; they are the ideas which recur to me, so to speak, every day and every instant of the day. To point out to men, if possible, what they ought to do to escape the tyranny and corruption implicit in democracy, such is, I think, the general idea which characterizes my book. . . . To labor in this sense is in my eyes a sacred occupation in behalf of which one should spare neither his money, nor his time, nor his life.[8]

In the United States it has often been taken for granted that Tocqueville was a great admirer of American democracy. The truth is somewhat different: what he admired was not American democracy, but the ingenuity of Americans in inventing political devices for mitigating the evils of democracy. In this, as in other respects,

[8] *Op. cit.,* V, 341.

Tocqueville was typical of nineteenth century Liberalism at its best. Like Lord Acton and Cavour and many another, he was an intelligent and humane lover of the masses, and yet a highly differentiated individual who prized his liberties, including the liberty of not belonging to the masses whom he loved.

Europe through the
Eyes of the Middle West

WHEN the war broke out in 1914, I was living, and for
a dozen years had been living, in Lawrence, Kansas. Lawrence, Kansas, is a thousand miles, more or less, west of
New York, and two thousand miles, more or less, east
of San Francisco; that is to say, it is in the heart of that
great agricultural inland region known as the Middle
West.*

The war came to us as a great surprise, but with no
great shock, because it seemed extremely remote, as remote almost as an Indian famine—something in which
we ought to take a decent and humane interest but with
which we would in the nature of the case never have
anything directly to do. The war was in Europe; and
with Europe we had most of us no contacts, nor had we
ever really known or seriously thought much about it.
To us Europe had at best no more than an academic interest. It neither affected our ordinary activities nor made

* An essay first published in *New Europe*, XV (May 13, 1920),
98–104.

a part of our cherished traditions. Besides, it was well established that the United States would never, under any circumstances, think it necessary or wise to "entangle our peace and prosperity in the toils of European ambition, rivalship, interest, humour, or caprice." For more than a century we had been repeatedly assured of this. Since we were so ignorant of Europe, it was comforting to know that indifference was a political virtue.

Not that our ignorance was complete. In our youth we had learned, at school, a little (such is the virtue of public schools) about the geography of Europe, a little about her history, a little about her present-day politics. We knew that Bismarck had founded the German Empire by "blood and iron." We knew that Italy was a kingdom, that its capital was at Rome, and that the Pope resided in that city. We knew that France had sent Lafayette to fight for us in the Revolutionary War, and that she had for some time been a Republic—two facts which disposed us to think well of her. We knew that Great Britain had a King, and that her Government was said to be democratic. How a monarchical Government could be democratic we did not know; but we knew that there had recently been some talk of abolishing the House of Lords—surely, we thought, a sensible thing to do. In the end it was not done, we never understood why. How could we? We had never had a House of Lords. Above all, we knew that Europe was a very old country, armed to the teeth, relatively poor, encumbered with the débris of outworn institutions, filled with ruined castles, and with Dukes who had seen better days and were proud of it. This we knew about Europe—an interesting place to visit, no doubt, but not a place one would wish to live

in; we wished it well, but were not over sanguine. Europe had never had our advantages.

With this knowledge we had commonly been content; but now the *Kansas City Star* poured over us such a flood of information about Europe that we began to suspect the school books of having unduly simplified the geography and politics of the old world. During the first months we read about the war with great interest, but with some confusion as to the precise issues, and with vague notions as to the location of the various places mentioned in the despatches. We took down the old school "geography" and rediscovered Liége and Luxembourg, Louvain, Mons, and the Marne. With some surprise we noted that Paris was well towards the north, really no great distance from the frontier—these European countries were so incredibly small! We wondered why this open frontier had not been fortified, until one day we read in the *Kansas City Star* all about the "neutralization" of Belgium. We had never heard of the neutralization of Belgium, which seemed, moreover, not in complete accord with what we had been taught about the sovereignty of States. We read with avidity, and we learned a great deal. The Pan-Slav menace and the Pan-German conspiracy, the Triple Alliance and the Triple Entente, Morocco crisis, *Mittel-Europa,* and Bagdad—all these became familiar abstractions to us, names which we could conveniently use to discuss the war in general terms. No doubt the precise content of these abstractions remained somewhat vague; but we soon learned enough to make up our minds on the main point, which was that Germany was the aggressor and ought to be defeated. In this settled conviction we went about our affairs hoping that the war would soon

end, believing that the Allies would win, impatiently relegating to the fringe of consciousness any suggestion that the United States would find it necessary to take a hand in the business.

Such suggestions came from time to time. From one source and another we learned that "down east" in New York and New England people were more excited about the war than we were. In the nature of the case we could not be well informed on public opinion down east. The United States is a large country, without any political or intellectual centre. President Wilson finds it necessary to get out of Washington to learn what the people are thinking about. Washington is not a good place for that. Neither Boston nor New York is much better. In fact, no place is a good place to be in if you wish to keep in touch with public opinion throughout the country; wherever you are in the United States you feel isolated. And so we only gradually learned what they were thinking down east. We did not read the *New York Times,* or the *Washington Post,* or the *Boston Transcript.* If by any chance we ever saw a copy of any of these papers it was two days late. No one likes to read old news; and therefore we got most of our news from the *Kansas City Star.* But from one source and another we found out that down east they were saying that, on grounds of interest as well as of morality, the United States ought to join the Allies. We learned that they were growing sarcastic about the crass "materialism" of the Middle West; the Middle West, they said, had no cities in danger of bombardment. In 1916 a distinguished vistor from the east told us that he confidently expected, within the year, to see German shells falling on New York; and about the

same time a friend of mine in Harvard University sent
me an outline map of the United States, marked 1920,
with boundaries drawn along the Allegheny and Rocky
Mountains, the Atlantic coast showing as German and
the Pacific Coast as Japanese colonies. Was he in earnest,
or only jesting? We could not be sure. The east was a
long way off; and we knew that it was in many respects
peculiar.

Perhaps the people down east were right after all; at
least we could see that the submarine campaign brought
the war nearer. We did not think we were "too proud to
fight"; but we had great confidence in the President, and
we noted that if he was too proud to fight he was apparently not too proud to make preparations for a fight if
it were thrust upon him. On the whole we were willing
to take our stand where he took it in the "Sussex" note.
We therefore helped to re-elect the President in 1916,
not, as was afterwards said by those who were too irritated to be dispassionate, because he had "kept us out of
war," but because we trusted his leadership, knowing that
if he gave the word for war it would be only after having
exhausted every reasonable means of preserving the peace.

When he gave the word we rallied, as the whole country rallied, to his support with great unanimity, accepting
conscription with scarcely a murmur, oversubscribing
the loans. The rapidity and success with which the Government placed a great army in France was, all things
considered, a remarkable achievement; it was more than
Europe expected of us, more than we expected of ourselves. The explanation is that the war, which we as
a people had not thought our affair and which we had
wished to keep out of, was accepted, when it came, as

a bad job which could not be shirked and which must
be thoroughly done. "We've got to put it over," is how
the average man expressed his attitude. This job was, in
terms of camp slang, to "can the Kaiser"; in terms of
pulpit and political oratory it was to stand unselfishly
at Armageddon in defense of an imperilled world. And
as we warmed to this job our former habit of detachment, our consciously preserved "neutrality in thought
and deed," rapidly gave place to a war psychology of the
most pronounced type. What enabled us to accomplish
much in the material conduct of the war was the exalta-
tion which permitted us to conceive it in the spirit of a
crusade.

Three things contributed to raise us thus suddenly to
a high pitch of intransigence. The first was no more than
that military patriotism which war always develops. When
we saw "the boys" march away under the flag, still more
when we saw them brought back maimed, or learned
that they were lying dead "somewhere in France"—then
the war became for the first time a reality to *us*. But, and
this is the second point, it was a reality which ought not
to have been ours; we were not directly or remotely
responsible. It was, so we still thought, a European affair,
of which the conditions were prepared by the ambitions
of European chancelleries, and for which the immediate
cause was the criminal and sinister designs of Germany:
a European folly, really, in which circumstance beyond
our control now involved us. We went into the war
with something of the exasperation of a man who per-
forms an altruistic action, not voluntarily, but because
the conventions of a situation which he did not create
impose it upon him. If we had to get Europe out of a

mess, we wished to do it thoroughly, so that it would never have to be done again. We wished this one exception to our traditional policy to be the one exception. We went into the war, therefore, determined to destroy the hateful thing called German militarism, believing at the same time that a war to end German militarism was the same thing as a war to end war.

The war to end War! This was the master phrase that justified war to an unmilitary people. The President's splendid formulation of the objects for which the Allies were fighting, his captivating vision of the regenerated world that was to emerge from the conflict—this above all was what enabled us to conceive of the war as a supreme spiritual adventure. As a people we heard the new gospel gladly. Some there were who remained skeptical, proclaiming the Fourteen Points visionary and absurd; some remained skeptical, but held their tongues, well knowing the value of apt phrases for achieving victory. Many —a noble company of intelligent and generous spirits— accepted the President's doctrines in all seriousness, aware that many obstacles would attend their practical application, but still believing that they corresponded to a possible, a practically manageable, reality; confident to the last that out of this ghastly collapse of civilization there would, because there must, emerge a new and better international order.

Yet all these made a small minority. The mass of the population, we whom Lincoln called the "plain people," welcomed the President's doctrines, if not less sincerely, at least less reflectively; we assented to them less with our minds than with our emotions. For us the President's fervid idealization of the war satisfied a profound psy-

chological need. It reconciled all contradictions between Right and Might, war and peace, the gospel of Christ and the gospel of force. It eased the burden of parents called upon to send away their sons. It enobled the motives of men who gave their days to the pursuit of gain and their evenings to putting the Liberty Loan drive over the top; of women who knitted while they drank tea and idly gossiped; of shop-girls who, munching chocolates at the play, experienced an unwonted emotion at the sight of Old Glory on the screen. The President appealed powerfully to that deep-seated sentimentalism which we like to feel but are ashamed to reveal; he prepared a rôle for us in which we could enjoy the illusion of playing a noble part without feeling foolish. And so we listened to the President and applauded him, as we listen to the minister who, on Sunday morning, declares the Sermon on the Mount to be the true rule of life— and for the same reason; not because these doctrines expressed our apprehension of reality, but because they formulated an ideal which we like others to think of us as having exemplified. In this high mood we fought the war.

Scarcely had we got used to this mood when the war suddenly ceased and left us without an object appropriate to it. We have found it difficult to divest ourselves overnight of our war psychology, to drop suddenly down from the exalted mood to our former complacent good humour; the consequence of which is that many of our official and self-constituted leaders, deprived of the German menace upon which to expend an accumulation of heroic and self-righteous emotion, have been busily engaged in turning up lesser menaces at home. These

they find everywhere in the guise of aliens who preach
the proletarian revolution, Socialist deputies who hold
opinions "inimical to the best interests of the country,"
college professors who dispassionately discuss the institution of private property, school teachers who are said
to read the *Nation,* the *New Republic,* and the *Dial.*
They tell us that the world must be made safe for democracy at home as well as abroad. And they find a
measure of support because we resent that anyone, especially aliens, should criticise our beloved institutions
at the moment when they have, as it seems to us, stood
the supreme test, or question the motives and enthusiasms
which during the war won us the admiration of humanity,
and which still enable us to feel complacent in a disillusioned world. We do not wish to be disillusioned; and
so our exalted mood is giving place to irritation, to
spasmodic outbursts of petulance, and puerile talk, and
purposeless persecution.

But what do we think of the Treaty? Frankly, we don't
think of it. The war is over, and all our purposes achieved.
The Kaiser is down and out, German militarism is
crushed, the Treaty of Versailles provides for the Allies,
so we are told, adequate guarantees against future aggression, and the League of Nations is set up to inaugurate
a new international order. We did our job well, as we
think; we are once more out of Europe; and we wish
to get back to business as usual. Our main thought about
the Treaty is, therefore, to wish that it may be ratified
and got out of the way. It makes us uncomfortable to
think about Europe, which we understand less than we
did before the war. Besides, we do not like to think. That
is why we have so many organizations, societies, clubs, as-

sociations, and committees of all kinds—to save us the trouble of thinking. In politics our political parties serve this purpose. At present our Republican leaders tell us that we must have reservations to the Treaty, although they are not agreed on that; and our Democratic leaders tell us that the Treaty is right as it is, although some of them think not. This confuses us; and so we say to the President and the Senate: "Get together and ratify the Treaty, with or without reservations as may be necessary; but at all events ratify the Treaty and make an end of the war."

I do not speak of the various small minorities that are for one reason or another interested, as they always have been, in European affairs—journalists, preachers, college professors, the educated and travelled classes, the politicians, the *internationales* of finance and big business and labour. These think of the Treaty, are for or against it, and write and preach and discuss and propose; they are aware of Europe, of its desperate situation, and of the need of something being done. But they make little headway against the millions that count, intellectually, for inertia—the stolid and comfortable well-to-do, the uneducated and untravelled poor, the idle rich, ignorant and replete with unassimilated experiences. Since June, 1917, I have been living in the East; and in September, 1919, I had occasion to go west to Waterloo, Iowa, the home of my youth. There I met relations and old friends of the family—physicians, lawyers, bankers, teachers, preachers, retired farmers, undertakers, grocers—representative citizens of this city of 30,000 people. During the five days I was there no one mentioned to me either Europe, or the war, or the Treaty of Versailles, or the

League of Nations, or the Senate, or the President. No one, except one woman who asked me: "Are you in favour of this League they are talking about?" I replied that I was not. "Well, I don't know that I am either," she said; "but all the rest have made peace, and I think they ought to fix it up somehow."

After all, Europe is remote, and its affairs very complicated. We have put the old "geographies" back on the shelf, and the exact location of Liége and Lauvain, of Mons and the Marne, is again becoming somewhat vague in our minds. It is true that to the boys who fought in France, and who still speak interestingly of these places, Château Thierry will always be more than a name, and Paris something other than a black spot on the map.

The Dilemma of
Liberals in Our Time

*Liberty is the right to do what-
ever does not injure others.*

TIME was, not so long ago, when the word "liberal"
went about the world in shining morning face, proud of
its achievements, confident of its future. Today, none so
poor to do it reverence, it peers cautiously out of door-
ways, shuffles along the shadow of walls, slinks around
corners into side streets. Our smartest radicals suspect it
of being an *agent provacateur* of Capitalism, while conservatives of ancient lineage treat it as a Bolshevik
masquerading in a rented dress coat. In an atmosphere
so forbidding is it any wonder that the battered word
should be manifestly ill at ease? It timidly joins this
group or that, puts questions that are rarely answered,
perhaps ventures, with friendly deprecatory gesture, some
or other remark to the effect that, all things considered, it
has nevertheless never been entirely convinced. Or else
it stands unobtrusively in corners hoping for the best—
hoping, but with every appearance of not expecting, to

catch sight of at least one smiling, good natured friend of former days. Lo, the poor liberal! What is the explanation of his present so diminished state? *

I

The liberal creed, in its most naïve and inclusive form, comes to us as a heritage from the eighteenth century. In that expansive and generous age it appealed to men of all classes (even nobles and priests having some superficial and temporary use for it), but it was best adapted to the uses of the enlightened bourgeois. The middle-class man, conscious of his virtues and ambitious to rise in a world where royal tyranny and class privilege cribbed him in on every side, found it convenient to be brightly optimistic and fell into the habit of believing that all men, or at least the great majority, were, like himself, naturally good, or would be apart from ignorance, bad laws, and the stigma laid upon them by the kings and nobles who ruled and exploited society in their own interests. This simple doctrine he found conveniently and cogently expounded by the *philosophes*—the Voltaires and the Rousseaus; and from them also he learned, what he most wanted to know, that God had intended

* A lecture with this title was originally given at the Columbia University Summer School in 1932. The essay here printed is the most complete of five versions in the Becker Papers, some titled as above or simply as "Liberalism." The essay was first published in part as "Liberalism—A Way Station," *Saturday Review of Literature,* IX (Dec. 3, 1932), 281–282; reprinted in *Everyman His Own Historian* (New York: Crofts, 1935), 91–100. The present version is printed by permission of *The Saturday Review,* Appleton-Century-Crofts, and the Cornell University Library.

all men to be free—every man free to learn what the open book of nature might teach, free to form and to express such opinions as reason might dictate, free to share in the choice of representatives who would enact into law the decisions of the common will, free to engage in any occupation, art, or craft that might be suited to his talent or agreeable to his temperament.

In short, the eighteenth century bourgeois, hampered by arbitrary and senseless restraints, naturally believed in liberty. And why indeed should not any man believe in liberty, a thing that, quite apart from particular restraints, was so desirable in the abstract, a thing moreover so easily definable and understood: liberty—that is to say, "the right of everyone to do whatever does not injure others." Equal rights of others, certainly: there would be no trouble about the others. The others would have their liberty too, the same liberties; so that, obviously, equality would emerge, automatically one might say, as a by-product of liberty. Once abolish the tyranny of kings, the privileges of nobles, the vested humbug of priests, and what would be left? Obviously, liberty and equality, the obverse of tyranny and privilege, would be left. A new world would be left, a world in which liberty and equality would go hand in hand in a friendly way, without disputing over priority or leadership. In this easily imagined world every reasonable and virtuous man would follow his inclination and pursue his interest without interfering with the right of all other reasonable and virtuous men to do the same. The new world imagined by the first liberals was as simple as that, or nearly so.

Meanwhile slow-footed time brought many changes, and with changes much revealing experience. The French

Revolution came, sweeping away old privileges, engendering furious fanaticisms and hatreds, bequeathing to the world its partial achievements, its hopes deferred, its fears and disillusionments. And then, following hard on, came Napoleon, grandly endeavoring to reorganize the European world in terms of "careers open to talent": grandly endeavoring, but ending at last in defeat and collapse. A quarter century passed—twenty-five years of revolution, war, upheaval, construction and reconstruction. The year is 1815. A strange world has emerged, but not the world imagined by the pre-revolutionary liberals: the old world not yet dead, the new still powerless to be born. The Castlereaghs and the Metternichs have finished at Vienna, not too well satisfied with their work there, but conscious of having done the best they could. Divine right seems still intact in Germany, but perturbed ministers send heavy-footed *gendarmes* into university classes, or anxiously scan lists of books withdrawn from libraries by professors. In France Louis XVIII reigns, but sits precariously balanced on his patched up throne, ruling under the limitations of the Charter and the Civil Code. In England gloomy Tories surround the half-demented king, with apprehensive Whigs on the lookout; and the Iron Duke and the Right Honorable Earl of Liverpool and all the lesser defenders of property and religion breathe more freely now that the Corsican adventurer is safely guarded at St. Helena. The Revolution is ended they think: international republicanism, that menace to civilization, has at last been beaten down and got under— so at least they hope. Yet they sleep but fitfully, and what dreams come to trouble their waking hours! There, outside, is the mob listening to Orator Hunt. There is mad

Shelley, writing seditious verse. And there, across the Channel in France, in no one knows how many knapsacks and secret cupboards, is the powder-stained but still flaming tricolor. The defenders of the old order think on these things and wonder if the Revolution is indeed ended.

II

They were quite right to wonder. Far from being ended, the Revolution was no more than well begun; and during the next three quarters of a century it made its way, gradually and by diverse methods indeed, with many compromises in theory and many concessions in practice, throughout western Europe. "It is evident," wrote De Tocqueville in 1835, "that a great democratic revolution is going on among us." It is still more evident today. From the vantage point of 1932 we can see that this democratic revolution was the outstanding political event of the nineteenth century; for whereas in 1789 the prevailing form of government was the absolute monarchy, supported by a privileged nobility and justified by the doctrine of Divine Right, in 1889 (if we must have a date) the prevailing form was government through representative assemblies, elected by a more or less democratic suffrage and justified, explicitly or tacitly, by the doctrine of the sovereignty of the people. Throughout all this long time the public issues which chiefly engaged statesmen and publicists were these: To what extent shall the people be permitted to share in choosing their rulers? What is the best form of government—the absolute or the constitutional monarchy, the bourgeois or the democratic

republic? What, in any case, are the proper functions of government, what are the rights properly reserved to the individual? How can the powers of government and the rights of the individual be adequately defined and definitively guaranteed in constitutional forms? One might say that the chief occupation of statesmen and publicists of that time was the manufacture of constitutions, the construction of locked vaults and strong rooms for safeguarding the rights of the individual. The legal emancipation of the individual from class or corporate or governmental restraint—this was the democratic revolution noted by De Tocqueville. To be a conservative was to be, with whatever qualifications, opposed to such emancipation; to be a liberal was to be, with whatever qualifications, in favor of it.

Conservatives, in every country, were chiefly upper-class—the privileged aristocrats, and their ecclesiastical and bureaucratic hangers-on, who had been or would be dispossessed by the democratic revolution. Wishing to retain or to recover their privileged position, they endeavored to "conserve" whatever had been or might still be kept of the old regime. Liberals, in the most general sense of that term, were the middle- and lower-class people who stood to gain by the democratic revolution; but the liberals, according to class interest or temperament, were themselves divided into what may be called the moderates and the radicals. Radical liberals were chiefly lower-class working men, led by intellectuals (in England called Philosophical Radicals), that is to say, upper- or middle-class renegades who, pricked by ambition or a tender-minded humanitarianism, became the plumed knights of the people. Impatient souls for whom the Terror had

no terrors, the working men were likely to be of Jefferson's opinion that "the tree of liberty needs to be refreshed from time to time by the blood of patriots and tyrants." And so, on all the great revolutionary days, we commonly find them behind the barricades, in ragged pantaloons, with gory-kerchiefed heads, armed chiefly (if we may trust many a contemporary print) with spades and daggers, with fife and drum, fighting the king's soldiers on behalf of the democratic republic of '93.

Occupying a middle ground between conservatives and radicals were the moderate liberals—chiefly middle-class business and professional people, with whom were associated many little white-collar proletarians and no small number of dislocated or un-class-conscious aristocrats. Having forgotten nothing and learned much since 1789, the moderate liberals were wise in their generation. They remembered the ideals of the great revolution, but had not forgotten the Terror. Their motto was therefore the golden mean, nothing in excess: they cherished the magic word "compromise." They would have freedom, but not license: no more autocracy, no more inherited privilege, but likewise no more mob rule, no more barricades: neither the tyranny of kings nor the tyranny of the unwashed. They would destroy privilege, but without endangering property. They would have government by the people, but by the best people—let the people who own a country govern it, as John Jay said. Liberty by all means, but a measured and restrained liberty. Occupying a middle ground between Not-Enough and Too-Much, the moderate liberals fought on two fronts, winning from kings and nobles liberties which they hoped to defend against the people. In that maladjusted world lumbering

along towards democracy, the function of the moderate liberals was to enable the aristocrats to ride comfortably in the tumbril unannoyed by a too unseemly hooting from the mob.

The difference between moderate and radical liberals seemed to contemporaries vastly important, but to us it seems a small matter, being chiefly a dispute as to whether liberty could be best guaranteed by a democratic or a ten-pound suffrage. The liberal creed made no such distinction, and to the liberal creed both moderates and radicals subscribed. Drafted by utilitarian economists and reduced to classic form by John Stuart Mill in his works *On Liberty* and *Representative Government,* the mid-nineteenth century liberal creed was not quite the same thing as its eighteenth century prototype. These hard-headed if forward-looking utilitarians painlessly cut away from the traditional doctrine most of the mystical and naïvely optimistic tenets so dear to the age of Enlightenment. They retained as a matter of course enough idealism to contend successfully with kings and nobles, and to keep alive, even if precariously, the hope of better things to come for the masses; but their principal achievement was to adapt the liberal creed to the material interests of the businessmen and bankers who rode to power on the swelling tide of the industrial revolution. Liberty was still defined as the right to do whatever does not injure others; and what did or did not injure others was still to be defined by law, that is to say, by the decision of the common will, however the common will might be registered in ballot boxes. The things one could do that did not injure others were of course many. For example, one could acquire sufficient property and intelligence

(even Mill admits that liberty is not for people or peoples in their "nonage") to share in choosing those representatives who would decide what did or did not injure others. The best way to acquire property, apart from inheriting it, was to engage in any legitimate business and make as great a profit as possible by buying in the cheapest and selling in the dearest market available. Free competition—this too, as well as political freedom and freedom of speech and religion, was one of the natural rights proclaimed by the great revolution; or, if the phrase "natural rights" stuck in the throat, one of those privileges so clearly demonstrated by Bentham to be useful to society. At a much later date Cecil Rhodes announced: "Philanthropy is all very well, but philanthropy plus five percent is a good deal better." This was the firm foundation of mid-nineteenth century liberalism, that it rested securely on philanthropy plus five percent: it united liberty and competition in the holy bonds of wedlock, made liberty useful by setting it up in business, and sanctified competition by anointing it with the incense of human freedom.

With this battery of principles the lower and middle classes gradually edged their way into the political fortress hitherto held exclusively or chiefly by the landed aristocracy. It was proper, by any decent rule of precedence, that the wealthy and well-to-do should enter before the common man, and no more than to be expected that, once in, they should endeavor to shut the gate in the face of the common man who had helped them to force it; so much so, that it became almost a conventionally recognized formula for easing in democratic government that the middle classes should have the aid of the masses

in breaking into the country of the aristocrats, and then the aid of the aristocrats in keeping the lower-class rascals out. For all that the lower-class rascals were admitted to the "political country" sooner than might have been expected. If the moderate liberals enjoyed a certain advantage in fighting on two fronts, it was a disadvantage to them that the liberal principles with which they fought were better adapted to winning privileges than to keeping them. Who could maintain with a straight face that God had created precisely that kind of a world in which political liberty could be properly defined in terms of a ten-pound suffrage? Besides, even the moderate liberals believed in "progress," and the implication of all their arguments was that some fine day the people would be sufficiently enlightened to govern themselves. Thus it happened that the very doctrines employed by middle-class liberals to unseat the aristocrats were employed by the advocates of democratic suffrage to break down the resistance of the middle classes.

Nevertheless, as it turned out, the entrance ways to the political country were opened to the people by those within rather than forced by those without. It was not that the middle classes wanted democracy, but that the middle-class political leaders could do with more votes. The Reform Bill of 1867, which extended the suffrage to working men in towns, was put through by Disraeli and Gladstone, neither of whom had any faith in democratic government, but each of whom was more than willing, in behalf of his own party, to give the illiterate the right to vote in the lively hope that the illiterate could be induced to vote the right ticket. Similarly in other countries. The French constitution of 1875 was not the

creation of the people, but a device of Orleanist mon-
archists and moderate republicans to mobilize popular
sentiment against Bourbons and Bonapartists. And it was
the arch-conservative Bismarck who made a gift of universal suffrage to the German people: "a species of
political blackmail" levied in the interest of German
unification, he afterwards explained; but Lassalle tells
us that at the time Bismarck was chiefly influenced by the
belief that the democratic suffrage would strengthen the
Conservative rather than the Liberal party.

Conservatives got the worst of that bargain. The word
"liberal" still had magic in it: even in the age of militant
nationalism, that time of "blood and iron," of blood
drawn by the sword in payment for blood drawn by the
lash, all was still thought to be done in behalf of freedom:
so that the lower classes, once given the vote, were
disposed to follow middle-class liberal leaders, convinced
that in voting the Liberal ticket they were somehow
striking a blow for freedom. Never, therefore, was the
prestige of liberalism higher than during the last decades
of the nineteenth century: when, in Germany, the great
Bismarck found it necessary to truckle to the National
Liberal party in order to make his imperial government
a going concern; when, in France, the liberal parties of
the center rallied in defense of the republic against
the multiplied menaces of Royalism, Clericalism, Boulang-
ism, Dreyfusism, Militarism; when, in England, the
Grand Old Man disestablished the Irish Church, endeavored in vain to push Home Rule through a Liberal
House of Commons, in vain to abate the scramble for
the liberty of exploiting and civilizing backward countries.

This Indian Summer of liberal content proved nevertheless to be no more than a brief season. For in truth, with the establishment of democratic government, with all the famous liberties formally conferred upon the individual, with the individual legally emancipated from class and corporate and governmental restraint, the great role of nineteenth century liberalism was ended, leaving liberals, like Othello, without occupation. Since no party any longer defended the divine right of kings or the hereditary privileges of nobles, where was the enemy? Now that all parties accepted democratic government as an accomplished fact, and all statesmen loved the common man, sufficiently so at least to solicit his vote, and even the priests, as Georges Sorel said, "claim to be the best of democrats, . . . have adopted the *Marseillaise* as their party hymn, and if a little persuasion is exerted . . . will have illuminations on the anniversary of August 10, 1792," a liberal might be excused for asking what, precisely, were the distinguishing marks of a liberal? Paraphrasing Polonius, he might well say: "What is it to be a liberal if it be not to be not a conservative?" What indeed! Yet to be not a conservative called for dexterity. In a world so rapidly progressing a liberal statesman's first care was obviously to keep well abreast of the times, or else fall behind in the procession and suffer the dreadful mischance of being mistaken for a reactionary. Not being always able to recognize his principles at first sight, it behooved him, every morning bright and early, to survey the situation anew, on the chance that he might find it expedient, before sundown, to accept as genuinely liberal something which yesterday he had, rightly enough, rejected with disdain. Thus it

happened that liberalism, once a passionate battle cry
in the warfare against royal oppression and class privilege,
fell to the level of a party slogan, while the genuine
eloquence of the prophets and crusaders of democracy
was transmuted into the plangent rhetoric of politicians
soliciting votes on the hustings.

Meantime, unknown to politicians of course, and quite
apart from the falsetto rhetoric of their Punch and Judy
show, the insistent question of human welfare was silently
assuming a new form. The prophets of democratic government had supposed that when liberty entered equality
would as a matter of course come trailing affectionately
along. But it was not so. When liberty appeared equality
was nowhere to be seen. Liberty had scarcely been made
welcome, therefore, before it was necessary to set out
in search of equality. It was this new aspect of the ever-
lasting adventure that disconcerted liberals, all but
dissolved the Liberal parties, and deprived liberalism of
that high prestige which it had formerly enjoyed.

III

Not the least important tenet of nineteenth century
liberalism was that the individual should be free in his
economic no less than in his intellectual and political
activities. *Laissez-faire,* free competition—what a wealth
of subtle dialectic was employed to demonstrate the
validity of these cleanly kept but unfurnished concepts!
Under any circumstances free competition would no
doubt have worked to the advantage of the intelligent, the
fortunate, and the unscrupulous. But what accentuated
this result, what the early prophets of freedom could not

foresee, was the industrial and technological revolution —that is to say, the amazingly rapid application of power-driven machinery to industry and the arts of life. The results of the technological revolution, superimposed upon a regime of free competition, were far more profound and disturbing than those of the political revolution. Briefly stated they were: (1) to increase enormously the production of wealth in the world; (2) to establish, in ways that no one could foresee or control, an intricate and close-woven economic interdependence between individuals, communities, and nations throughout the world; (3) to place a very great part of the wealth of the world in the hands, or at the disposal, of those persons, relatively few, who by intelligence, luck, or lack of scruple, managed to obtain control of the machines and instruments of production; and accordingly (4), to give to the possessors of machines and the instruments of production a power over governments, over the manufacture and dissemination of information, and over the lives and fortunes of the mass of the people which would have reduced dead and gone kings and nobles, could they have imagined it, to envious admiration. Before the end of the nineteenth century it was obvious to the discerning that democracy had belied the hopes of its prophets. Instead of bringing in peace and good will, enlightenment and justice, an equitable distribution of wealth, and the spirit of fraternity, it had brought in, or at least had failed to keep out, political corruption, industrial brigandage, social oppression for the masses, and moral and intellectual hypocrisy on a scale rarely equaled and perhaps never surpassed. In short, liberty, that liberty for which liberals had so valiantly fought, had

ironically given birth to a brood of mean-faced tyrants, and, so far from walking hand in hand with equality, was to be found consorting chiefly, and secretly, with puffed and bedizened privilege.

The first to feel the new oppression were the industrial workers. For some years, convinced that they could obtain higher wages and shorter hours by "collective bargaining" (strikes and lock-outs managed by labor unions), they were content to vote with the old upper-class parties, conservative or liberal as the case might be. But strikes proved expensive and too often unsuccessful, and it became every year more apparent that the old parties were interested in the laboring man in order to get his vote rather than to do him any real service. Sooner or later, therefore, the industrial workers organized political parties of their own: the German Social Democratic Labor Party (1875); the Belgian Socialist Party (1885); the Austrian Social Democratic Party (1888); the French United Socialist Party (1905); the British Labor Party (1906)—to name only a few of them. These new parties had all the same object—to obtain for the workers in particular, and for the mass of the people in general, a more equitable share in the social income. They had all much the same practical program of immediate social reform—laws imposing restraints on employers in the interests of laborers, laws taxing the rich in the interest of the poor. And they had all much the same social philosophy. This philosophy, formulated by Karl Marx, came to be known as scientific socialism. Briefly, scientific socialism announced the coming social revolution, the result of which would be the abolition of the competitive system by the "socialization" of land and capital—that is to say, by

placing in the hands of the government (which would somehow be controlled by the people) the ownership of the means of production and the control of the distribution of wealth. Not *laissez-faire* but socialization, not a competitive but a regulated economy, not individual liberty for individual profit but restraint of the individual for the welfare of all—such was the new gospel of socialism which arose to confront and contend with the old gospel of liberalism.

Threatened by the rising power of socialism, with its revolutionary doctrines and its anti-liberal program, the possessing classes closed their ranks. All the decayed landed aristocracies of Europe (English Tories, French Royalists, German Junkers), which the political revolution had deprived of their former privileges, united with the new aristocracy of bonded bourgeois wealth, which the industrial revolution had created, to defend the new regime of liberal democracy. They were now all good conservatives, since they wished to conserve the existing regime; all good liberals, since the regime they wished to conserve was the one which for a century liberals had heralded and fought for. Thus the industrial revolution aligned the classes against the masses; and this alignment was accompanied, in the political arena, by a new alignment of parties. On the Right were the conservative parties of ancient lineage, strengthened by recruits from the *nouveau riche,* defending the regime of democracy and free competition. On the Left were the new proletarian socialist parties, proclaiming the social revolution and fighting for social reform and a regulated economy. In the Center stood the old liberal parties. What were they proclaiming? What defending?

With liberal conservatism to the right of them, and revolutionary socialism to the left of them, the old-fashioned liberal had three choices—all disagreeable. He could poke his head in the sand. He could modify his principles and mildly socialize his program, thus (as a "Progressive Liberal") progressively edging over to the Left in order to fight unanticipated evils. Or he could stick to his traditional principles, join the unsavory company of his ancient enemies, and find himself derided as a renegade apologist of oppression. Some chose one line, some another; many availed themselves of all three according to the need of the moment. Generally speaking, big-business liberals were most likely to contract the habit of voting conservative, while little-business liberals crept under the sheltering wing of the socialist parties; thus leaving a corporal's guard of leaders, professional people and intellectuals to hold the liberal fort, as always on two fronts. This process of dissolution was well under way in continental countries before the Great War. In England it is only recently that the great Liberal party of Gladstone has dropped to third place. For some years now its chief function, as J. M. Keynes so well says, has been to serve the state by supplying the Conservative party with leaders and the Laborites with ideas; and we need not wonder that it has at present so few of either, having in the last quarter century lost so many of both.

Of all the leaders lost to the Liberal party, the most notable is undoubtedly Ramsay MacDonald, whose career throws a brilliant light on the predicament from which all genuine liberals now strive with indifferent success to extricate themselves. Aristocratic in his avocations and in his demeanor, he lives by preference the life of a gen-

tleman and a scholar. Inheriting the Scot's canny cau-
tion, deliberative by temperament and thoroughly rooted
in British tradition, he understands the high virtue of
compromise and has always set his face against violence.
Nevertheless, being eminently humane, he has always
preached social reform on behalf of the poor. Being eminently reasonable and reasonably ambitious, he calls
himself a socialist and has risen to power as the leader
of the Labor party. And yet through all the vicissitudes
of an exciting career he has managed to retain the liberal
point of view, watching his step both ways, often uncertain whether to be counseled by his conscience which
bids him budge with the masses, or by the Fiend who
bids him budge not with the classes: the upshot of which
is that he has been three times Prime Minister, and today,
deprived of a party, stands in splendid isolation, dis-
creetly holding a faded socialist flag and courageously
leading a Conservative House of Commons. All this is
but an abstract and brief chronicle of liberalism in our
time.

Before the Great War this hunting with the hounds
and running with the hare was not too difficult. Contend-
ing desperately for votes, the socialist parties moderated
their doctrine and the liberal parties socialized their program so expertly that no substantial distinction between
them was visible to the naked eye. Between the liberalism of Lloyd George and the socialism of Ramsay Mac-
Donald, there was not in the great days of 1910, the
difference of the twentieth part of one poor scruple. That
is no doubt why, in those days, we all (all, in that in-
determinate sense, good liberals, good socialists) admired
them both. But the practical implications of the socialist

doctrine are now fast becoming real issues. The Marxian, communist, anti-liberal revolution has actually occurred in Russia; the Fascist, anti-democratic revolution has occurred in Italy. Both appear to be in the way of accomplishing their objects. We have only to remove our heads from the sand to see, on the arena of western civilization, the issues sharply defined, the conflict realistically staged: on the one side a ruthlessly regulated economy, such as we see it in process of establishment in Soviet Russia or Fascist Italy; on the other a free competitive economy (made workable by whatever patchwork of socialistic devices) such as we see it functioning in France, Great Britain, and more especially in the United States. Looking at these contrasted systems in the long perspective, one may say, at the risk of oversimplification, that whereas the chief trend of the nineteenth century was to emancipate the individual from social oppression, the chief trend of the twentieth is likely to be the emancipation of the masses from oppressions (more properly perhaps confusions) incident to unrestrained individual activities. In this view, liberalism may be regarded as a by-product of democracy, and democracy itself as a passing phase, a loose and extravagant method of government practicable only in relatively simple agricultural societies suddenly dowered with unaccustomed wealth by the industrial revolution; while equalitarianism may be regarded as a by-product of highly complex, interdependent technological societies working inevitably, and no doubt impersonally, towards uniformity and equilibrium. Throughout the nineteenth century, liberty and equality, commonly appearing coupled and inseparable in theoretic discourse, were mistaken for blood brothers; in the twen-

tieth century, by the pressure of events dissociated and made to confront each other with hostile intent, they are seen to be enemies of long standing. Both profess to be good democrats, friends of the people; but whereas liberty still affirms, perhaps with some loss of confidence, that under free democratic government, the individual can take care of himself, equality declares dogmatically that no government can be democratic that fails to take care of weak and unfortunate individuals, even against their will, by protecting them against the strong and the unscrupulous.

As this issue becomes more sharply defined, the predicament in which we liberals of the old-fashioned sort find ourselves becomes more pronounced, becomes even, if we wish to do anything about it, really pathetic. Our predicament arises from the fact that, having long been enamoured of both liberty and equality, we are now ever more insistently urged to choose between them; and the truth is that we cannot with clear convictions or a light heart choose either without the other. So we stand irresolute, pulled one way by our traditional ideals, another by our humane sympathies. As we are humane, thoroughly infected by Christian slave morality, we look with compassion on the "looped and windowed raggedness" of the poor, invoke on their behalf the sacred principle of equality, and secretly admire, at the safe distance of three thousand miles, the high Russian endeavor to apply it in practice. Yet we shudder at the thought of blood, and assure the Bolsheviks that the Great Society cannot be created by cutting off heads or suppressing the freedom of speech for which, in the distant past, so much blood was ruthlessly shed. Although humane lovers

of the masses, we are, on the other hand, highly differentiated individuals who prize our liberties, including the liberty of not belonging to the masses whom we love; and having long been unaccustomed to authority arbitrarily exercised, we hate Mussolini for the professors he has silenced, and write letters to the *Nation,* or else sign futile petitions, protesting in the name of liberty against his brusk tyrannies. Yet we find it impossible not to denounce, in our own country where we are still free to denounce them, those oppressions which have emerged under the aegis of the very liberty we invoke. Choose? Oh me, that word "choose!" We may neither choose what we would nor refuse what we dislike, so inextricably interwoven do they seem to be. We cannot choose liberty without denouncing the measures now taken to obtain equality, or choose equality so obtained without betraying liberty.

It will perhaps be said that liberty and equality are not irreconcilable, not really. It will be said (has been said often enough) that there is a "true" liberty which implies equality, and a "true" equality which implies liberty. True liberty and true equality—yes, I know them; I know them well—those two stately ladies, in immaculate robes, standing on pedestals, and between them a third, with bandaged eyes, holding the scales even. I know *them,* I love them too, I even make them a courtesy, wave them in passing a friendly greeting; but I do not embrace them since I know they are not real. My plight, the plight of all liberals, is that we are asked to choose between real, realizable, liberty, and real, realizable, equality. Real liberty and real equality we can often enough find in history. In the age of Pericles there was liberty—for citi-

zens; there was equality—among slaves. In the eighteenth century peasants enjoyed a measure of equality: nobles and priests defended their liberties—we call them privileges. Real liberty and real equality, as history reveals them to us—no goddesses are these, in immaculate robes, but buxom wenches that open doors and scrub floors. They stand not on pedestals. They work in houses, but in different houses: liberty is the handmaid of the fortunate, equality serves the lowly.

And so the gods that be, those wooden-faced croupiers at life's gaming table, issue their monotonous warning: "Make your bets, gentlemen!" Will you place your counters on the green or the red, on liberty or equality? One or the other. This is no game of heads I win, tails you lose. For myself, I choose the green, since I am more enamored of liberty than of equality. I would, were it possible, have both in their fullness; and I count myself fortunate indeed to have been personally favored almost equally by both, to have lived in a richly blest country where, time and place according, liberty and equality could temporarily live side by side as harmoniously as ever was, or perhaps ever will be, possible. But I prize the liberties I have more than I resent the inequalities to which I am subject. If I were standing in a bread line, it may be that I should prefer Russian equality with all its restrictions on liberty; being what I am I prefer American liberty with all its flagrant inequalities. In a bread line or out of it, I am by nature a non-conformist; the satisfaction of being a heretic without being a martyr is not easily overestimated. And so I place my counters on the green, on liberty; yet not with too great confidence, not without an appealing upward glance at the goddesses

on the pedestal, hoping for the best: hoping for the best, but well aware that the green may, and probably will, prove a losing game in the end.

One may as well bet on the outcome, there is no harm in that, since it is as likely a method of influencing the course of affairs as any other form of activity. At least if the green proves a losing game in the end it will not be because some one organized a new party, or because Mr. Thomas may live long enough to be elected President of the United States. It will be because at present the gods appear to cast a favorable eye on the common man and the machines, and the common man and the machines are placing their counters on the red. Unfortunately for us perhaps, the intellectual freedom which we so highly prize is of little concern to the average man, since he rarely uses it, while the freedoms he can make use of are of slight value to him. In our free democratic society the average man does indeed enjoy (if that is the word) many freedoms. I will note a few of them. He is free to read the amazing mixture of information and misinformation daily laid before him in newspapers managed for private profit and supported by business advertisements. He is free to turn a dial and listen to the melody of "The Bells of St. Mary" fade away into a sugary voice announcing that lemon pies are delicious—free, that is to say, to listen to radio announcers whose sentimental fabrications are designed to hypnotize him into buying something not needed or not worth having. He is free to buy a new car as soon as he has made the last payment on the car he possessed before the one he now desires to turn in. He is free to govern himself by voting for candidates selected for him by politicians who make a

living out of the spoils of office. He is free to take any job that offers, if any offers; if none offers, free to hunt for a job that, if found, will pay him a living wage, or less; if none is found, free to stand in a bread line begging a crust from charity, or from the government that makes him a free man. What is called the "competitive system" (ironic contradiction in terms) has enlisted a high degree of intelligence in solving the problem of the production and transportation of wealth, while the equally important problem of the kind of wealth needed and its equitable distribution has been left to chance; the result of which is a "system" (if you can call it one) so maladjusted that a bumper cotton crop ruins every one connected with the industry, and millions of people in the richest country in the world are undernourished because of an unfortunate "overproduction" of useful and useless commodities.

What the average man wants, much more than he wants the liberties we prize, is security; and he will support those who can and will give it to him. The average man scarcely understands liberty in our high sense. He likes of course to do as he pleases, but is strongly averse to being made responsible for what it is that he pleases to do. He is instinctively suspicious of eccentricity, and is nowise irked by conformity. Uniformity, the equality of mediocrity, gives him all the liberty he needs, since he is not measurably different from the great majority of people, and does not wish to be. Give him security, and within security the freedom to do and to think what everybody does and thinks—give him bread and circuses, bacon and automobiles—and he will not clamor for those political and intellectual liberties which we so desperately

cling to. And, unfortunately for us perhaps, the machines appear to be on the side of the average man. Having invented the machines, we must make the best of them. Master them we will, no doubt. Master them we do; but a prime condition of mastering them is that we should adapt our conduct to their necessities. To make the best use of them we must meet them more than half way, since they care nothing for us while we care greatly for them. It is the machines that make life complicated, at the same time that they impose on it a high tempo; and what the machines demand of the individual living in a closely intermeshed society running at top speed is not eccentricity, however cultivated and engaging, but conformity. The idle curiosity, the mental vagabondage of the brooding, reflective mind, the machines will indeed accept, but at discount rates only; they put a premium on the immediately realizable activities—on promptness, regularity, precision, effortless adaptability. Step lively, watch your step, keep your eyes on the red light, don't jay-walk—that is what the machines say. And today they are saying it to the capitalist as well as to the laborer. They are saying it to financiers and statesmen. They are saying it to college presidents and professors.

I began by calling attention to the word "liberal"— one of those magic words that have, on the world's stage, their entrances and their exits, playing meanwhile their brief parts. In conclusion I should like to call attention to another word that has recently made an unobtrusive entrance. The word is "planning." There has been much talk, round and round about, of constructive planning. Nothing very radical has as yet been suggested, nor has much been done, in that way. It has been suggested that

every third row of cotton be plowed under, and in one state the military has been called out to regulate the production of oil. In the way of constructive planning this is not much perhaps. But so much talk, and even any slight action by those in high places, indicates at least a certain awareness that what is needed in our messed-up industrial society is less liberty and more control, a less purely competitive and a more consciously regulated economy.

Are we then headed towards a more consciously regulated economy? I should think we are headed towards a more regulated economy, whether achieved consciously or by force of circumstances is another question. If we are headed towards a more consciously regulated economy, can we achieve it by other methods than those employed in Soviet Russia or Fascist Italy? We have liberty to plan. Have we also sufficient intelligence? I do not doubt that we have sufficient intelligence. The vital question is, will our intelligence be defeated by our liberty? Perhaps the high function of the confirmed liberal in our time is to be still free to hope that we may preserve our liberty to plan without making futile all our plans.

What Is Still Living in the Political Philosophy of Thomas Jefferson?

I believe . . . that there exists a right independent of force.—THOMAS JEFFERSON

MANY nations have traced their history back to a fabled Golden Age, to the beginning of created things, when, as Hesiod says, "men lived like Gods, free from toil and grief." Our own history can likewise be traced, through its European origins, back to that mythical time. But we commonly think of it as beginning more recently, somewhat abruptly, in the clear light of day, with the settlement of Jamestown, the landing of the Mayflower, and the founding of Massachusetts Bay colony. Men did not then live like Gods, or free from toil and grief; but there were in those days men of heroic stature, men around whom myths have gathered, and whom we delight, with good reason, to honor. The beginning of our history as an independent nation is still more recent,

and still more open to critical inspection in the still brighter light of the eighteenth century; and yet this is for us still more truly the time of our Golden Age, and of our ancestors of heroic stature. Among the founders of our federal republic (to name only the most distinguished) were Washington, Franklin and John Adams, Alexander Hamilton and John Jay, Robert Morris and James Wilson, Richard Henry Lee, James Madison, and Thomas Jefferson. No doubt we are apt to magnify these "Fathers" beyond their just merits. Their just merits were nevertheless, sufficiently great; for it would be difficult to find, in the history of any other country, or in the history of our own country at any other time, within a single generation, as many statesmen in proportion to the population equally distinguished for learning, probity, and political intelligence. And of these ten men, none exhibited these qualities to better advantage or more lasting effect than Thomas Jefferson.*

Jefferson, like Franklin, attained an international eminence; like Franklin he was familiar with all of the ideas of his time, contributed something to its accumulated knowledge, and was identified with its most notable activities and events. There was indeed scarcely anything of human interest that was alien to his curious and far-reaching intelligence. Nevertheless, his name is for us inevitably associated with a certain general idea, a certain way of regarding man and the life of man, a certain political philosophy. The word that best denotes

* An address given before the American Philosophical Society, April 22, 1943; originally published in *Proceedings of the American Philosophical Society*, LXXXVII (1944), 201–210; reprinted by permission of the American Philosophical Society.

this political philosophy is "democracy." More than any other man we think of Jefferson as having formulated the fundamental principles of American democracy, of what we now like to call the American way of life.

Any significant political philosophy is shaped by three different but closely related influences. The first is what Alfred North Whitehead has taught us to call the "climate of opinion"—those unconsciously accepted presuppositions which, in any age, so largely determine what men think about the nature of the universe and what can and cannot happen in it, and about the nature of man and what is essential to the good life. The second is more specific: it derives from the political conflicts of the time, which dispose groups and classes to accept a particular interpretation of current ideas as a theoretical support for concrete political measures. The third is still more specific: it derives from the mind and temperament of the individual who gives to the philosophy its ordered literary form. Whatever is original in the philosophy is usually contributed by the individual who gives it this form. Whatever value it has for its own time depends largely upon the extent to which it can be used to illuminate or resolve the particular political issues of that time and place. But its value for other times and places will depend upon the extent to which the fundamental presuppositions on which it rests have a universal validity—the extent to which they express some essential and enduring truth about nature and the life of man.

The political philosophy of Thomas Jefferson was not in its fundamental principles original with him. It was his only in the sense that he gave to ideas widely current,

and genuinely entertained by him, a Jeffersonian form and flavor. Nowhere is this peculiarity of form and flavor so evident as in the famous Declaration of Independence, but Jefferson did not claim that the ideas themselves were in any way novel. Some years later his old friend John Adams, a little irritated (as he was apt to be on slight provocation) by the laudation of Jefferson as the author of the Declaration, protested to Pickering that there "is not an idea in it but what had been hackneyed in Congress for two years before." [1] To this Jefferson replied that it was not his purpose "to find out new principles, . . . to say things that had never been said before, but to place before mankind the common sense of the subject," and to harmonize the "sentiments of the day, whether expressed in conversation, in letters, printed essays, or the elementary books of public right." [2] This was indeed Jefferson's merit, and the high value of the Declaration for his own time, that it expressed in lucid and persuasive form ideas then widely accepted, and thereby provided a reasoned justification for renouncing the authority of the British government. But the Declaration purports to have a higher value than that; for in providing reasons for renouncing the authority of a particular government at a particular time, Jefferson took occasion to formulate the universal principles that, as he believed, could alone justify the authority of any government at any time.

These principles are formulated in a single paragraph. We are all familiar with it, having read it or heard it read many times. But it will always, and certainly at no

[1] Charles Francis Adams, *Works of John Adams* II: 514. Boston, 1850.

[2] *Writings of Thomas Jefferson* (Ford ed.) VII: 304, 407, 1896.

time more than now, bear repeating; and I will therefore repeat it once more, not precisely as it appears in the Declaration, but as Jefferson first wrote it in the orignial draft.

We hold these truths to be sacred and undeniable; that all men are created equal and independent; that from that equal creation they derive rights inherent and inalienable, among which are the preservation of life, and liberty, and the pursuit of happiness; that to secure these rights governments are instituted among men, deriving their just powers from the consent of the governed; that whenever any form of government shall become destructive of these ends, it is the right of the people to alter or to abolish it, and to institute new government, laying its foundation on such principles and organizing its powers in such form, as to them shall seem most likely to effect their safety and happiness.

This statement contains the sum and substance of Jefferson's political philosophy, which may be reduced to four fundamental principles: (1) that the universe and man in it is governed by natural law; (2) that all men have certain inherent natural rights; (3) that governments exist to secure these rights; and (4) that all just governments derive their authority form the consent of the governed. These principles, made explicit in our federal and state constitutions, are still the fundamental principles of our political system; and on this anniversary occasion, when we are fighting a desperate war to safeguard the political system that Jefferson did so much to establish, it is indeed appropriate for us to ask: What is still living in this political philosophy? In order to answer this question, I will break it down into two more specific questions. First, what did Jefferson understand by natural

law and natural rights, and what form of government did he think best suited to secure these rights? Second, to what extent is his conception of rights and government still valid for us?

The doctrine of natural law and natural rights, as Jefferson understood it, was revolutionary only in the sense that it was a reinterpretation, in secular and liberal terms, of the Christian theory of the origin, nature, and destiny of man. As commonly understood in the eighteenth century, it was perhaps never better stated than by the French writer, Volney.

Natural law is the regular and constant order of facts by which God rules the universe; the order which his wisdom presents to the sense and reason of men, to serve them as an equal and common rule of conduct, and to guide them, without distinction of race or sect, towards perfection and happiness.[3]

For Jefferson as for Volney, God still existed. But for them God the Father of Christian tradition had become attenuated into God the Creator, or First Cause. Having originally created the world for a beneficent purpose and according to a rational plan, the Creator had withdrawn from immediate and arbitrary control of human affairs to the dim recesses where absolute being dwells, leaving men to work out their own salvation as best they could. But they could work out their salvation very well because the Creator had revealed his beneficent purpose, not in Holy Writ, but in the open Book of Nature, which all men by the light of reason could read and interpret. "Is it simple," exclaimed Rousseau, "is it natural that

[3] *Oeuvres* (second ed.) I: 249. Paris, 1826.

God should have gone in search of Moses in order to speak to Jean Jacques Rousseau?" To Rousseau, to Jefferson and Volney, it seemed more natural that God should have revealed his beneficent purpose through his works; from which it seemed self-evident that the whole duty of man was to discover progressively, by studying his created works, the invariable laws of nature and of nature's god, and to bring their ideas, their conduct, and their social and political institutions into harmony with them.

From this conception of natural law Jefferson and his fellows derived the doctrine that all men are created equal and are endowed by their creator with certain natural and imprescriptible rights. Many otherwise intelligent persons have thought to refute Jefferson by pointing out that all men are in fact not equal. With the same ingenuity and poverty of imagination one might refute St. Augustine's doctrine of the brotherhood of man by pointing out that all men are in fact not brothers. All men, St. Augustine would have replied, are brothers in the sight of God; and Jefferson's doctrine of equality comes to the same thing—that all men are equal in the possession of a common humanity, and if they are not in fact equal, and have not in fact the same rights and privileges, the highest morality, both for the individual and for society, is to act always on the assumption that all men should be accorded, so far as is humanly possible, the same opportunities and consideration. To act on this asumption would be, both for individuals and for society, to do the will of God and to live the good life.

In this respect—in respect to the primary values of life—the natural rights philosophy of Jefferson was

essentially at one with the Christian faith; but in respect to the means best suited to realize these values, it differed sharply for current official Christian teaching. It denied that man is naturally prone to evil and error, and for that reason incapable, apart from the compulsion of church and state, of arriving at the truth or living the good life. On the contrary, it affirmed that men are endowed by their Creator with reason in order that they may progressively discover what is true, and with conscience in order that they may be disposed, in the measure of their enlightenment, to follow that which is good. It was perhaps the dominant quality of Jefferson's mind and temperament, as it was of so many men of his time, to have faith in the worth and dignity, the rational intelligence and good will, of the individual man; and it was for this reason that, in considering the means for achieving the good life, they relied so confidently upon the negative principle of freedom of the individual from social constraint—freedom of opinion, in order that the truth might prevail; freedom of occupation and of enterprise, in order that careers might be open to talent; and freedom from arbitrary political control, in order that no man might be compelled against his will.

These freedoms were precisely what Jefferson meant by "liberty" as one of the inalienable rights of man, and it was through the fullest enjoyment of these freedoms that the "pursuit of happiness" would be most likely to end in happiness for the greatest number of men. And so we arrive at the central idea of the natural rights philosophy in respect to the proper function of government—the happy idea that the best way to secure the inalienable rights of man is just to leave the individual

as free as possible to enjoy them, and that accordingly
no form of government can secure them so well as the
one that governs least. This idea was so engaging that
anyone with an unbounded faith in the natural goodness
of men, and an equal faith in the validity of formal logic,
might easily push straight on to the conclusion reached
by Proudhon—the conclusion, namely, that "property is
theft," that all governments exist to condone it, and that
men will never be free and happy until all governments
are abolished.

Jefferson had not sufficient faith either in the native
goodness of men or in formal logic ever to reach that
conclusion. He had more faith in the goodness of men
than many of his contemporaries—more, for example,
than John Adams; but less than some others—less, for
example, than Samuel Adams or Thomas Paine. He had
a logical mind, and relied upon it, but logic was not for
him a "systematic way," as has been said, "of going wrong
with confidence"—not, that is to say, a device for
manipulating empty concepts in the void in vain, but
a means of reaching sound practical conclusions on the
basis of knowledge and common sense. History and political experience, rather than the logic of political theory,
convinced Jefferson that men had been governed too
much, and above all too arbitrarily, by kings claiming
divine right, and that among the institutions that ob-
scured the native goodness of men by depriving them of
equal rights none was less defensible than a hereditary
aristocracy enjoying privileges that were unearned and
exacting a deference that was unmerited. It seemed to
him self-evident, therefore, that the people could govern
themselves better than kings and aristocrats, whose powers

and privileges rested upon the accident of birth, could do it for them. Not that the people could govern themselves with perfection, or without difficulty. All forms of government, he was aware, had their evils, and of popular government the principal evil, he said, was "turbulence; but weigh this against the oppressions of monarchy, and it becomes nothing." [4]

The evils of government by the people were even less than nothing when compared with its virtues, its chief virtue being that "it is the only form of government that is not eternally at open or secret war with the rights of mankind." [5] But what, in concrete instances, did Jefferson mean by "the people" who have a right to govern themselves? The people, in this sense, might mean all the people in the world, or all the people in Virginia, or all the people composing a particular race or sect. Practical statesman that he was, Jefferson took the world, politically speaking, as he found it, divided into groups that by tradition and community of interest regarded themselves, and were commonly regarded, as "nations." For purposes of government, all such nations might at any time "assume, among the powers of the earth, the separate and equal station, to which the laws of nature and of nature's God entitle them." Thus nations as well as individuals had their natural rights—the right of political self-determination. But how was this self-determination to be effected, how was the consent of the governed to be obtained? Any nation is composed of individuals, and individuals necessarily differ in their opinions and their interests; and it seemed to Jefferson

[4] *Writings of Thomas Jefferson* (Ford ed.) IV: 362, 1894.
[5] *Ibid.* V: 147, 1895.

self-evident that the only practicable way of reconciling these differences was by majority vote. Even a monarchy with all of its trappings, or an aristocracy with all of its privileges, if really supported by a majority vote, would be a "just government" because it would rest on the "consent of the governed."

Not that majority vote conferred on the majority of the moment any fundamental right not shared by the minority. It was merely a practical device imposed upon individuals bound by their nature to live together, and aiming to live together with the maximum degree of harmony and good will; and Jefferson justified it by saying that this rule once disregarded, "no other remains but force, which ends necessarily in military despotism." [6] There is, of course, no more fundamental or obdurate problem in political philosophy than that of the conflicting interests of the one and the many—the difficulty being to reconcile the desirable liberties of the individual with the necessary powers of society; and Jefferson was not more successful than other philosophers in providing a satisfactory solution of it. His solution, such as it was, is presented in a letter to Dupont de Nemours,[7] some portions of which I venture to quote, because in it he states briefly and categorically, and better perhaps than anywhere else, the chief tenets of his political faith.

I believe with you that morality, compassion, generosity, are innate elements of the human constitution; that there exists a right independent of force; that the right to property is founded on our natural wants, in the measure with which we are endowed to satisfy these wants, and the right to what we acquire by those means without violating the

[6] *Ibid.* X: 89, 1899.   [7] *Ibid.* X: 24, 1899.

similar rights of other sensible beings; that no one has a right to obstruct another exercising his faculty innocently for the relief of sensibilities made a part of his nature; that justice is the fundamental law of society; that the majority, oppressing an individual, is guilty of a crime, abuses its strength, and by acting on the law of the strongest breaks up the foundations of society; that action by the citizens in person, in affairs within their reach and competence, and in all others by representatives, chosen immediately, and removable by themselves, constitutes the essence of a republic; that all governments are more or less republican in proportion as this principle enters more or less into their composition; and that government by a republic is capable of extension over a greater surface of country than any other form.

The right of national self-determination, and republican government based upon popular suffrage and majority vote—these were Jefferson's fundamental ideas as to the form of government best suited at any time and in any country to secure the natural rights of man. Turning then from the proper form of government to its function, we find that Jefferson would confine its activities within narrow limits. In the passage just quoted, and in Jefferson's writings generally, we can note his disposition to believe that man is naturally good but that men are prone to evil; or, translating it into political terms, that citizens in the mass are to be trusted but that citizens elected to office need to be carefully watched. I have quoted Jefferson as saying that the chief evil of republican government is "turbulence"; but he did not really think so. Indeed, he said that a little turbulence on the part of the people now and then would do no harm, since it would serve to remind elected officials that their

authority was after all only a delegated and limited franchise from the people. What Jefferson really believed is that political power is inherently dangerous, and that accordingly the chief evil in any form of government is that there may be too much of it. From this it followed that in devising a republican government the chief aim should be to avoid that danger by dispersing power among individual magistrates, separating it in respect to function, and otherwise limiting it by applying the grand negative principle of checks and balances. Fundamentally, Jefferson agreed with Thomas Paine, that whereas society is the result of men's virtues, government is the result of their vices, and therefore a neccessary evil: necessary in order to preserve order, protect property, and guarantee contracts; evil because inherently prone to magnify its authority and thereby impair the liberties of the individual.

Jefferson's ideal of democratic society and republican government could best be realized in a small agricultural community, such as he was familiar with at Monticello, composed of a few men of substance and learning like himself and his friend James Madison, and otherwise chiefly of industrious, upstanding yeoman farmers; making altogether a community of good neighbors, in which every one knew who was who, and what was being done and who was doing it. The affairs of such a community, being easily within the "reach and competence" of the people, could be managed by them with the minimum of officials, exercising the minimum of authority, and attended with the minimum of palaver and ceremonial display. Unfortunately, this ideal com-

munity could not live to itself; and since this was so it
was necessary for the people, in managing the affairs of
the wider region, to delegate their authority to representatives. This departure from the ideal was the
beginning of danger; but there was no help for it except
to prepare for the danger in good time by electing
representatives for very short terms and limiting their
powers to very specific matters.

The broad principle would then be that the wider the
area the less safe it would be to entrust representatives
with power; from which it followed that representatives
from the counties to the state capital of Virginia could be
safely entrusted with more power than could be safely
entrusted to the representatives from Virginia to Phil-
adelphia. That the states must remain united, Jefferson
fully realized; but he was convinced that the several
states must retain their sovereign powers, and at first
he thought the Articles of Confederation very nearly the
ideal constitution for such a union. When experience
proved that a "more perfect union" was necessary, he
approved of the Constitution of 1787, but insisted, as a
guarantee against too much power in the hands of a
government far removed from the people, that a bill
of rights should be incorporated in the Constitution, and
that the powers therein granted to the federal government should be strictly and narrowly interpreted.[8] As it
happened, Jefferson's grasp of political realities was
destined to override this principle. As President, he
pushed through the purchase of Louisiana in spite of the
fact that in so doing he was exercising an authority which

[8] *Ibid.* V: 41–42, 45, 81, 1895.

he believed the Constitution did not confer upon him.[9] That perverse circumstances should have made Thomas Jefferson the man to usurp power from the people is ironical enough, and it troubled his political conscience not a little; but he could reflect that he tried, although in vain, to get a constitutional amendment to authorize the act, and that in any case his conscience was clear since he had acted solely for the public good.

Closely associated with Jefferson's fear of the open usurpation of political power, was his fear of the secret and more insidious influences by which men become debased and corrupted. Republican government, he was aware, could not well succeed unless the majority of citizens were independent, honest, and reasonably intelligent. Intelligence could be sufficiently trained and directed by education—schools for the people and colleges for the leaders. But honesty and independence depended far less upon precept than upon the conditions in which men lived. The best conditions were those of country life. "Cultivators of the earth," Jefferson said, "are the most virtuous and independent citizens."[10] Vice and political corruption flourished, as he thought, chiefly in cities and the industrial communities that produce cities. In cities, where people were mostly unknown to each other, unscrupulous individuals could push their selfish

[9] Jefferson to R. R. Livingston, April 18, 1802 (*ibid.* VIII: 143, 1897). This is the letter in which Jefferson made his famous statement that if France took possession of New Orleans, "we must marry ourselves to the British fleet and nation." Today we are again marrying ourselves to the British fleet and nation, and for essentially the same reasons given by Jefferson in justification of his statement.

[10] *Ibid.* III: 279, 1894.

interests under cover of the general indifference; and industrial communities, making so much of impalpable and evanescent forms of wealth, opened the door to speculation for unearned profit, stimulated greed, and rewarded conspicuous but useless luxury: provided all the conditions, in short, for the rise of a corrupt and politically influential "money power." Jefferson regarded a limited commerce and industry as necessary adjuncts of agriculture, but he had the farmer's settled antipathy to banks and their dubious financial manipulations. "The exercise, by our own citizens, of so much commerce as may suffice to exchange our superfluities for our wants," he cautiously admitted, "may be advantageous to the whole"; but he was profoundly convinced that it would be fatal for us "to become a mere city of London, to carry on the commerce of half the world at the expense of waging eternal war with the other half." Capital invested in agriculture and useful manufactures was productively employed; but "all of the capital employed in paper speculation is barren and useless, producing, like that on a gaming table, no accession to itself"; and as for banks, they are "a blot left in all our constitutions, which, if not covered, will end in their destruction." [11] Jefferson was never weary of pointing to England as the most ominous example of a nation rapidly losing its freedom by the unchecked multiplication of such evils; and he was convinced that the United States would suffer the same loss if it did not profit in time by that example.

Such in brief was Thomas Jefferson's political philosophy—his conception of human rights, and of the particular form of government best suited to secure those

[11] *Ibid.* X: 28, 1899.

rights. What then is still living in this philosophy? To what extent is Jefferson's conception of rights still valid for us? To what extent is the form of government recommended by him well adapted for securing the rights, whatever they are, that need to be secured in our time?

Any careful study of Jefferson and his ideas is apt, sooner or later, to leave one with the general impression that he was more at home in the world of ideas than in the world of men and affairs. He had little of Franklin's salty zest for life in the rough, little of his genial, tolerant acceptance of men as they are, and none of his talent for being comfortable in crowds and hobnobbing with persons of every station, from kings to scullions in the kitchen. Jefferson was a democrat by intellectual conviction, but by temperament and training a Virginia aristocrat—a man of cultivated tastes and preferences, with a fastidious aversion from what is vulgar and boisterous, passionate and irrational and violent in human intercourse. One may say that he felt with the mind as some people think with the heart. John Adams said that his writings were characterized by "a peculiar felicity of expression." [12] They were indeed—perhaps a little too much so. In reading Jefferson one feels that it would be a relief to come, now and then, upon a hard, uncompromising, passionate sentence, such as: "As for me, give me liberty or give me death." What one expects to find is rather: "Manly sentiment bids us to die freemen rather than to live as slaves." Jefferson's ideas had also this felicity, and also perhaps a little too much of it. They come to birth a little too easily, and rest a little precariously on the aspirations and ideals of good men,

[12] Charles Francis Adams, *Works of John Adams* II: 514, 1850.

and not sufficiently on the brute concrete facts of the world as it is. Jefferson was no visionary, and in his policy in respect to the purchase of Louisiana he exhibited a masterly grasp of international political realities; but it is characteristic of him that, in respect to the Embargo, he should have taken the position that our neutral rights, since they were in theory equally violated by France and England, should be impartially defended against both countries, even though England alone was able to do us any injury in fact; characteristic also that the high intention of his method of defending those rights was to attain the object by humane and peaceful means, and its signal effect to inflict a greater material injury on the United States than it did on the countries by which our rights had been violated. One suspects that with a little more humane feeling and a great deal more passion in his make-up, Jefferson would have been an out-and-out non-resistance pacifist; as it is he presents us with the anomaly of a revolutionist who hated violence, and a President of the United States who was disconcerted by the possession of political power.

If Jefferson was more at home in the world of ideas than in the world of men and affairs, it follows, more or less as a consequence, that, as a political philosopher, he was a better judge of ends than of means. In all that relates to the fundamental values of life, both for the individual and for society, in all that relates to the ideal aims that democratic government professes to realize, his understanding was profound. But in respect to the means, the particular institutional forms through which these values and ideal aims were to be realized, he was often at fault, if not for his own time at least

for the future. And when he was at fault, he was so partly because he conceived of society as more static than it really is; partly because he conceived of American society in his time as something that could, by relatively simple political devices, be kept relatively isolated and with slight changes be preserved in its relatively Arcadian simplicity. But his chief limitation as a political philosopher (and one should in fairness remember that it was the chief limitation of most political thinkers of his time) was that he was unduly influenced by the idea that the only thing to do with political power, since it is inherently dangerous, is to abate it. Jefferson did not sufficiently recognize the harsh fact that political power, whether dangerous or not, always exists in the world and will be used by those who possess it; and as a consequence of this failure he was too much concerned with negative devices for obstructing the use of political power for bad ends, and too little concerned with positive devices for making use of it for good ends.

This gives us, in general terms, the answer to our questions. In respect to fundamentals, Jefferson's political philosophy is still valid for us; in respect to what is more superficial—in respect to certain favorite institutional forms—it is outmoded. In elaborating this general answer I can note only the salient points.

None of Jefferson's ideas are so irrelevant to our needs as those about banks and speculation, cities and industrial communities—not because there is not much truth in what he had to say about them, but because his hope that the United States might be kept a predominantly agricultural society was entirely misplaced. During Jefferson's time there was occurring, insidiously and

without blare of trumpets, a revolution of which he was unaware, or the profound significance of which at all events he quite failed to grasp. I refer of course to the Industrial, or more properly the Technological, Revolution occasioned by the discovery and application of steam power, electricity, and radiation. It is now obvious that this was one of the two or three major revolutions in the history of civilization. Within a brief span of years, by giving men unprecedented power over material things, these discoveries have transformed the relatively simple agricultural societies of the eighteenth century into societies far more complex, more integrated, and at the same time more mobile and swiftly changing than any ever known before—formidable, blank-faced leviathans that Thomas Jefferson would have regarded as unreal, fantastic, and altogether unsuited to liberty and equality as he understood those terms. That Jefferson did not foresee this momentous revolution is no discredit to him; no one in his time foresaw it more than dimly. But the point is that the societies created by this revolution are the societies in which we live, and in connection with which we have to consider anew the nature of human rights; and it is not obvious that the favorite doctrine of Jefferson and of his time, the doctrine of *laissez-faire* in respect to economic enterprise, and therefore in respect to political policy also, can no longer be regarded as a guiding principle for securing the natural rights of men to life, liberty, equality, and the pursuit of happiness.

The doctrine of *laissez-faire,* as it was understood by Jefferson and the early nineteenth-century social philosophers, rested upon the assumption that if each individual within the nations, and each nation among

the nations, attended to its own interests, something not themselves, God or Nature, would do whatever else was necessary for righteousness. Or, better still, as Professor Edward H. Carr has put it in his recent book, the doctrine was based on the assumption that from the unrestrained pursuit of individual self-interest a "harmony of interests" would more or less automatically emerge.[13] In the political realm this meant that the function of government should be limited in principle to the protection of life and property, the enforcement of contracts, the maintenance of civil order, and the defense of the country against aggression. In the economic realm it meant that the free play of individual initiative, stimulated by the acquistive instinct, would result in the maximum production of wealth, and that the competitive instinct, operating through the price system, would result in as equitable a distribution of wealth as the natural qualities and defects of men permitted. In the international realm it meant that the strict attention to national interest and power by each sovereign state, restrained by the recognized rules of internaional law, would tend to create a balance of interests and of power which would serve, better than any other method, to promote international commercial exchanges and cultural relations and to preserve the peace.

It is now sufficiently clear that this doctrine of *laissez-faire*—of letting things go—however well adapted it may have been to the world in which Jefferson lived, is no longer applicable to the world in which we live. In a world so highly integrated economically, a world in which the tempo of social change is so accelerated, and the

[13] *The Conditions of Peace:* 105, 1942.

technological power at the disposal of individuals and of governments is so enormous and can be so effectively used by them for anti-social ends—in such a world the unrestrained pursuit of self-interest, by individuals and by states, results neither in the maximum production or the equitable distribution of wealth, nor in the promotion of international comity and peace, but in social conflicts and global and total wars so ruthless as to threaten the destruction of all interests, national and individual, and even the very foundations of civilized living. In our time the right to life, liberty, and the pursuit of happiness can be secured, not by letting things go and trusting to God or Nature to see that they go right, but only by deciding beforehand where they ought to go and doing, so far as possible, what is necessary to make them go there. The harmony of interests, if there is to be any, must be deliberately and socially designed and deliberately and co-operatively worked for. To bring this harmony of interests to pass is now the proper function of government; and it will assuredly not be brought to pass by any government that proceeds on the assumption that the best government is the one that governs least.

The history of the United States for the last hundred years confirms this conclusion, and nullifies for us Jefferson's favorite idea that the function of government should be reduced to a minimum, that sovereign rights should be retained by the states, and that the powers of the federal government should be strictly and narrowly interpreted. Decade by decade the states have gradually lost their sovereign powers, and the federal government, by virtue of a liberal interpretation of the Constitution and of amendments to it, has assumed powers that have

been used to limit the freedom of some individuals in order to protect the freedom of others. This extension of power and expansion of function on the part of the federal government has been brought about, in spite of the inertia of traditional ideas and the pressure of interested groups, by the insistent need of regulating the activities of powerful corporations which, although regarded in law as private enterprises, are in fact public utilities, and which therefore enjoy irresponsible power which they are sometimes unwilling but more often unable to use for the public good. It is in this respect that the engaging word "liberty" now appears in a guise unknown to Jefferson and his contemporaries. In the eighteenth century the obvious oppressions, for the majority of men, were those occasioned by arbitrary governmental regulation of the activities of the individual; so that liberty could be most easily conceived and understood in terms of the emancipation of the individual from social constraint. But in our time the principle of free enterprise has created a situation in which the obvious oppressions, for the majority of men, are those that arise not from an excess of governmental regulation but from the lack of it; so that liberty can now no longer be understood in terms of political and economic *laissez-faire,* but only in terms of more and more intelligent social regulation of economic enterprise. Jefferson and his contemporaries, as James Bryce has well said, "mistook the pernicious channels in which selfish propensities had been flowing for those propensities themselves, which were sure to find new channels when the old had been destroyed." [14] The selfish

[14] *Modern Democracy* I: 14, 1921.

propensities with which we have to deal are the same as they were in Jefferson's time; but since the channels —the institutions and customs—in which they flow are different, the remedies must be different also.

In this respect—in respect to his idea of the proper function of government—the philosohhy of Jefferson is now outmoded. But this is after all the more superficial aspect of Jefferson's philosophy; and if we turn to its more fundamental ideas—the form of government as distinct from its function, and the essential rights to be secured as distinct from the specific means of securing them—we find that Jefferson's political philosophy is as valid for our time as it was for his.

That the republican form of government—that is to say, government by elected representatives and magistrates—is the best form Jefferson was convinced because, as he said, it "is the only form of government that is not eternally at open or secret war with the rights of mankind." The republican form of government, which Jefferson helped to organize under the Constitution of 1787, still exists essentially unchanged; and today we accept it with even less qualification and divided loyalty than obtained in Jefferson's time. We accept it for many reasons, no doubt—because it has on the whole worked so well, because we have become habituated to it, and because there is nothing in our political traditions to provide us with a model of any other form. But we also accept it for the same fundamental reason that Jefferson accepted it—from the profound conviction that it is the only form of government that is not at war with the natural rights of mankind, or at all events with those familiar rights and privileges which we regard as in

some sense natural because from long habituation they seem to us imprescriptibly American.

Recent events have greatly strengthened this conviction. Some twenty years ago we were in a mood to ask whether the representative system of government might not be, if not at open, at least too often at secret war with the rights of mankind. That was a mood induced by comparing the democratic practice with the democratic ideal, with the inevitable if perhaps salutary result of magnifying the defects and minimizing the virtues of the democratic system as a going concern. But for ten years past we have been permitted, have indeed been compelled, to reappraise the democratic system with all of its defects in the light, not of the democratic ideal, but of the practical alternative as exhibited for our admiration in Germany and elsewhere; and the result of this reappraisal has been to make it clear that the defects of our system of government are after all, in comparison, trivial, while its virtues are substantial. Indeed, the incredible cynicism and brutality of Adolf Hitler's way of regarding man and the life of man, made real by the servile and remorseless activities of his bleak-faced, humorless Nazi supporters, has forced men everywhere to reexamine the validity of half-forgotten ideas, and to entertain once more half-discarded convictions as to the substance of things not seen. One of these convictions is that "liberty, equality, fraternity," and "the inalienable rights of man" are generalities, whether glittering or not, that denote realities—the fundamental realities that men will always fight and die for rather than surrender.

It is in defense of these rights, and of the democratic or republican form of government, that we are now

fighting a desperate war; and we justify our action by the very reasons advanced by Jefferson—that the democratic form of government is the form best suited to secure the inalienable rights of man. We may be less sure than Jefferson was that a beneficent intelligence created the world on a rational plan for man's special convenience. We may think that the laws of nature, and especially the laws of human nature, are less easily discovered and applied than he supposed. We may have found it more difficult to define the rights of man and to secure them by simple institutional forms than he anticipated. Above all, we have learned that human reason is not quite so infallible an instrument for recording truth as he believed it to be, and that men themselves are less amenable to rational persuasion. Nevertheless, in essentials the political philosophy of Jefferson is our political philosophy; in essentials democracy means for us what it meant for him.

Democracy is for us, as it was for him, primarily a set of values, a way of regarding man and the life of man. It is also for us, as it was for him, a set of concrete institutions devised for the purpose of realizing those values. We understand, as he did, but rather more clearly than he did, that the concrete institutions are bound to change: they have changed in many ways since Jefferson's time, they are changing now, and they will change even more in time to come. But we may believe, as Jefferson did, that the essential values of life are enduring; and one reason for believing so is that the values which we cherish are those which Jefferson proclaimed, and which for more than two thousand years the saints and sages of the world have commonly regarded as the ideal end

and ultimate test of civilized living. If we were to write a modern declaration of the democratic faith, it might run somewhat as follows:

We hold these truths to be self-evident: that the individual man has dignity and worth in his own right; that it is better to be governed by persuasion than by force; that fraternal good will is more worthy than a selfish and contentious spirit; that in the long run all values, both for the individual and for society, are inseparable from the love of truth and the disinterested search for it; that the truth can be discovered only in so far as the mind of man is free; that knowledge and the power it confers should be used for promoting the welfare and happiness of all men rather than for serving the selfish interests of those individuals and classes whom fortune and intelligence have endowed with a temporary advantage; and that to secure these high aims in the life of man no form of government yet devised is so well adapted as one which is designed to be a government of the people, by the people, and for the people.

To this declaration of the modern democratic faith Thomas Jefferson would, I feel sure, have subscribed without qualification. And it is in this sense, the most important sense of all, that his political philosophy, and still more the humane and liberal spirit of the man himself, abides with us, as a living force, to clarify our aims, to strengthen our faith, and to fortify our courage.